Introduction

Start with blank walls. Turn the gallery over to a large group of artists working independently of each other. Keep ground rules to a minimum. Lay on a large supply of black markers and operating room-issue booties as shoe covers. Let the artists go wild.

This is how Scrawl began at Artspace: as a seven-week exploration and experiment, a game with an indeterminate outcome that was in many ways so bold and unpredictable that I suspect not many museums or galleries would have been willing to try it.

There were precedents, of course, from the caves at Lascaux to the pulsating wall drawings of Sol LeWitt, and, in Artspace's recent past, an exhibition organized by Stephen Grossman entitled On The Wall (adopting some of the strategies of Gordon Matta-Clark). However, none had offered the potential for unleashing glorious anarchy inherent in forty-four artists coming face to face with 5,000 square feet of virgin space.

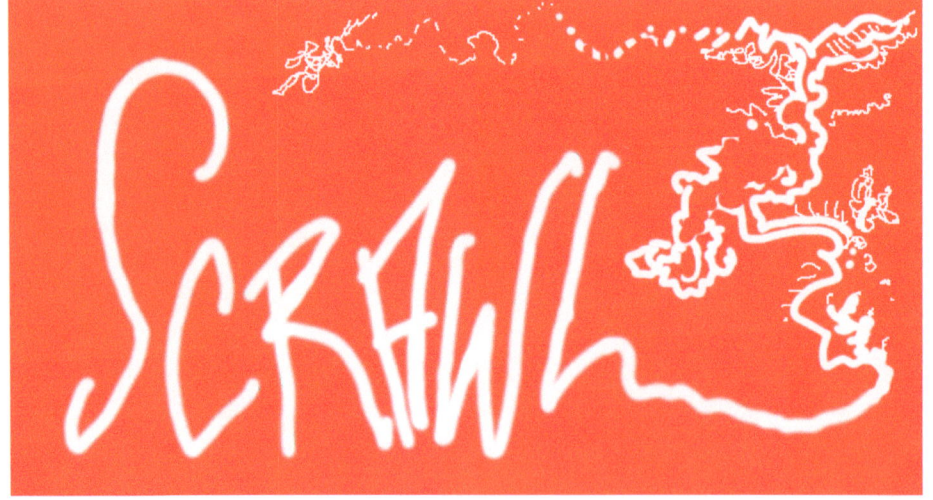

Artspace has always been a place that relishes artistic risks, where artists can try out an idea or test a concept, and in Martha Lewis, who masterminded this giant game through a series of brilliant tactical moves, we found a fearless collaborator.

What was most striking about the wonderful weeks in which Scrawl spread across our space was the way in which Artspace was transformed—and I mean spiritually even more than visually—into a lively community studio. Artists would stop in on their way to their day jobs to clear their heads with some time at their walls, or conversely, after a day's labor, to segue into evening. Those of us working in the Artspace office would check in too, providing moral support and enjoying a peek at the morphing drawings. On many occasions, the artists' friends would come by to take stock and add to the coterie of boosters and supporters hanging out. Even without the addition of some old couches, Artspace was transformed into a lively studio, a buzzing center of activity. And throughout, the great equalizer was the blue hospital booties that we all wore—artists, staff, and audience alike—to ensure the floor works were protected.

The impact of Scrawl on the artists and on Artspace was as much political as visual. To borrow a notion espoused by fellow organizer Matthew Stadler, whose Publication Studio focuses on building DIY communities of book-making, the game of Scrawl was an inherently political action: a way to mobilize audiences, to conjure up a curious crowd that might otherwise only come at the end—or perhaps not at all—and thus galvanize a public into being.

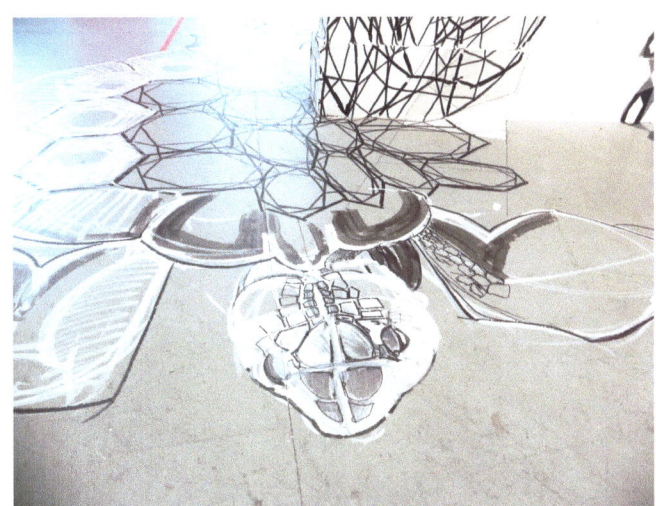

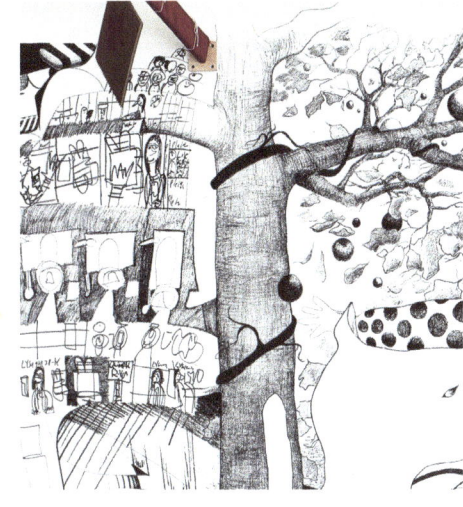

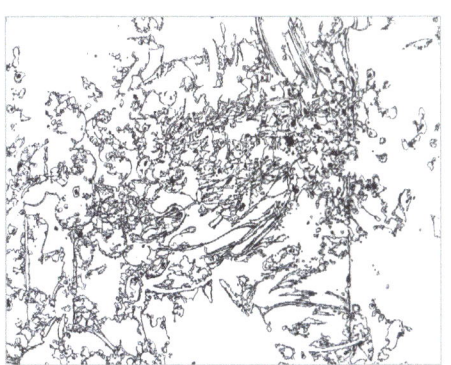

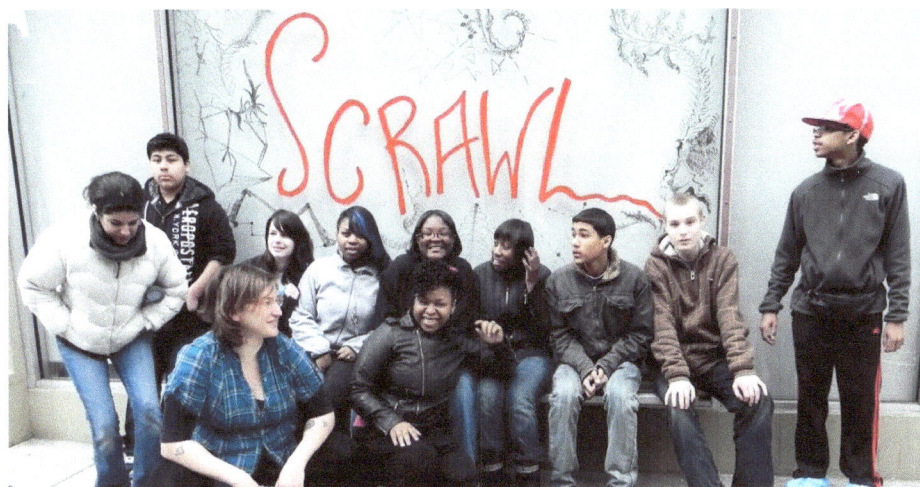

For me, memorable highlights included taking a yoga class under the graceful lines of Melissa Marks's variation on her ongoing Adventures of Volitia, its dynamism energizing all thirty-five yoga practitioners as we held our moves and performed salutations, while Scrawlers and other life-drawing artists drew our poses. A workshop that brought veterans participating in the Veterans Administration Hospital's Post Traumatic Stress Disorder art therapy to Artspace to hone their drawing skills and stretch their sense of themselves as a creative force. The teams of young people from Coop Arts & Humanities High School who worked with visiting English artist Rebecca Salter to create their section of wall using weather patterns and street life observable through Artspace's windows. The Futurists, a team of students from Educational Center for the Arts who divided into specialized worker sub-units—students who focused on minute, abstract and repeating shapes versus others who laid down an apocalyptic landscape. And a class of eighth graders from Betsy Ross School who prepared their own exquisite corpse creatures with Scrawler (and Betsy Ross alumna) Alexis Brown.

As Scrawl's conclusion drew near, something magical happened. Artists blended the edges of their works with those of their neighbors, and the most imaginative of connections were made. Cat and mouse games of whimsical provocation led artists to embellish and add some final flourishes, perhaps in the hopes of gaining the upper hand or just relishing the chance to delight in the joys of fully embodied drawing, which, after all, was our deepest hope for this project.

An unveiling, cast as "The Big Reveal," was a rousing finale to the many weeks of labor and heralded the so-called end. With visitors posing against various backdrops to have their photos taken—engaging with the work as tourists might in front of famous frescoes and murals—the transformation of Artspace into a new forum for art was complete. As I look back, I can proudly say that Scrawl exceeded, in both its visual manifestation and its community impact, even our wildest expectations.

—Helen Kauder, Executive Director, May 2011

Shifting from terra incognita to terra firma

As an experiment in exploratory drawing, Scrawl can be described as a kind of mapping, a spanning of the space through embodied mark-making, claiming territory, negotiating borders, issuing challenges and parlaying treaties. At once competitive and cooperative, over time the terra incognita of the white walls and grey floors morphed into terra firma, giving artists ownership of the space. Every corner, every electrical outlet, every lump, unevenness, every edge, became intimate, known, incorporated. This marking of space over time, this occupation of the exhibition arena, using diagrammatic flat lines to conquer the three-dimensional reality of the galleries, was at once a race, a contest, a laugh, and sometimes an arduous journey through a wilderness of mental and physical trials.

It was also really fun.

Its official title was Scrawl: Drawing Writ Large. A tall order with huge ambitions and little to show at the beginning except a lot of gallery space hung with bright red rip-stop nylon curtains. This was my first big project in the gallery, and one I hoped would catalyze its participants into making something expansive and wonderful.

I conceived of Scrawl as a way to invest artists in the organization, invert the traditional modes of exhibition, and privilege the gallery space itself as the target of interest. I wanted to construct a temporal project that would linger, that would have a quiet but profound impact on the participants' studio practices, long

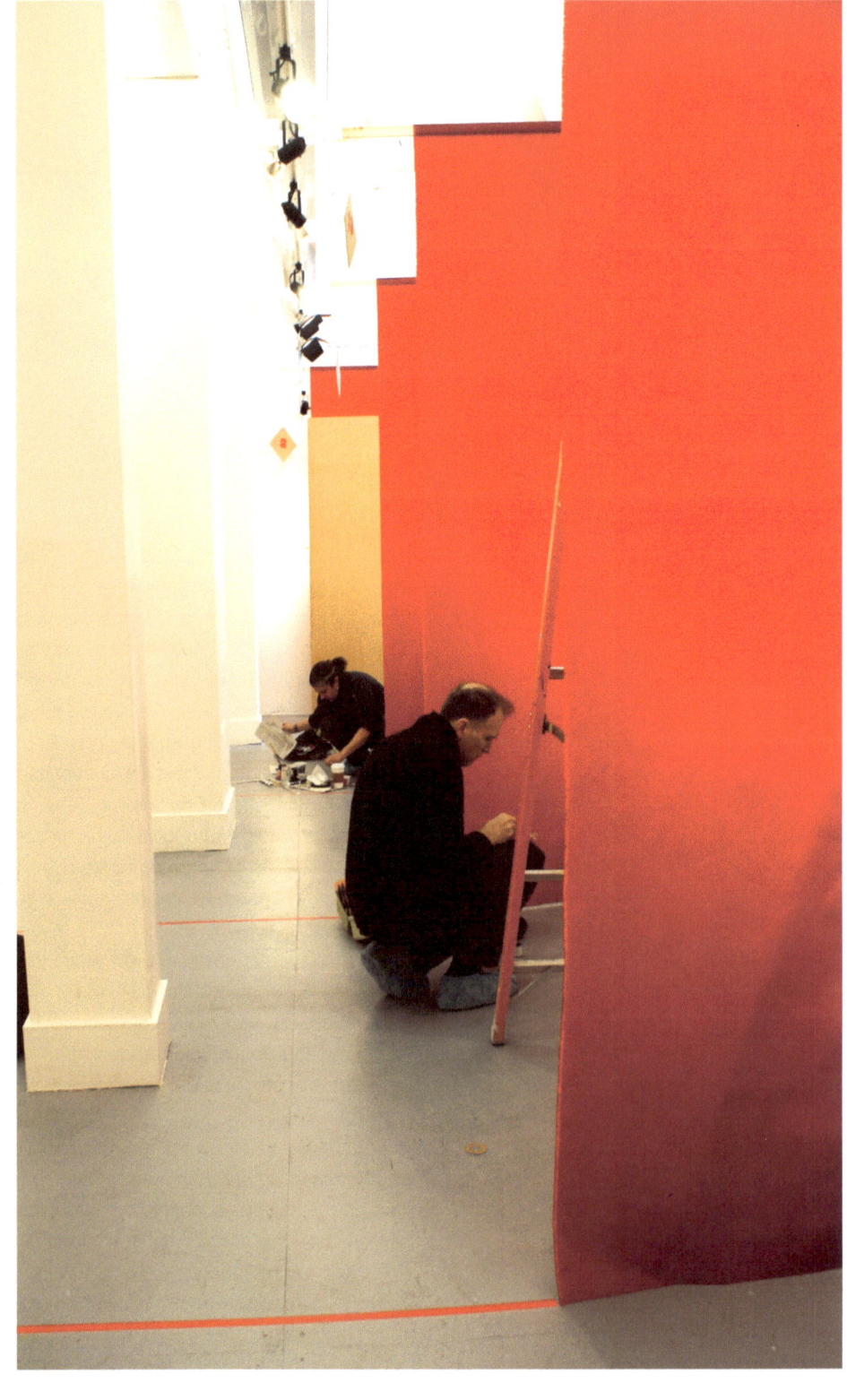

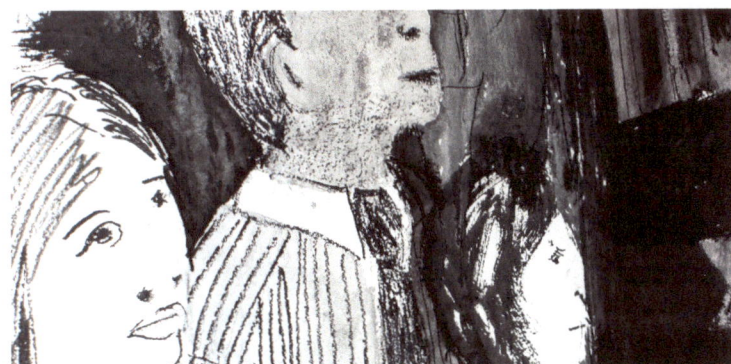
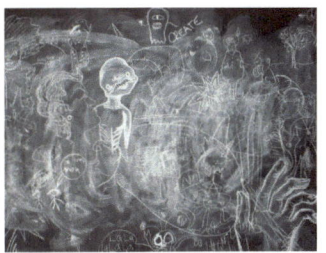
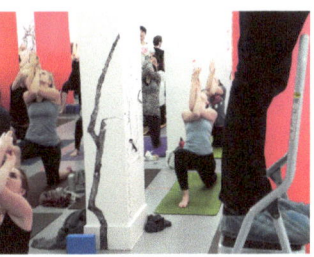

after the project had ended, vanished. This was an exhibition about what one can do with minimal means and a time limit. There is no doubt that it was challenging for the artists, difficult and daunting as much as exhilarating and liberating. It required bravery to make marks so publicly and with so few opportunities for disguise or prevarication: the mark was laid bare. This was the hard part, so simple, but so charged.

The artists who participated generously gave their time and talents, putting elbow grease, love, and thought into their work, their main reward being the experience itself. This event was complex to organize, as are all games that involve so many participants, and like all really good games, there was play, but it was serious play.

On February 9, 2011, forty-seven artists began working, individually and in teams, to transform the terrain of Artspace with simple materials and their own ingenuity. A drawing project inspired by the Surrealists' exquisite corpse games, Scrawl created an exhibition in an experimental way with minimal means—Sharpie markers and the gallery's topography. Scrawl was an embodied drawing-based initiative with a visually undetermined outcome.

We had seven weeks, twenty-two artists and teams, and nine feet of space per artist/team; work was allowed on walls, floors, and windows. I selected the forty-seven participants to include artists at various stages of their careers, and with as wide a range of drawing approaches as

possible. We added to the surreal mix with cool gear: staff and interns acting as game "referees" wore shiny sheriff's badges, and to protect the gallery floors during Scrawl, keeping them clean enough to draw on, we asked all who entered the space to don blue surgical booties. At once reviled and grudgingly adopted, these booties appear in every image, becoming one of the icons of the show and, later, a fond memory. Having the work be in black and white let things be ornate without being too chaotic, giving a consistency across the terrain of the galleries.

The traditional exquisite corpse, as practiced by the Surrealists, was a literate and visual game, which imposed strictures to create randomness, disconnect, and loss of aesthetic control in an exercise to privilege the unexpected, unforeseen, and unpredictable. Being a large-scale version of this, Scrawl created its own set of problems, as the scale shift altered the precepts considerably.

Despite our side curtains and panel screens, it was all but impossible to truly mask off the space while still retaining accessibility for visitors. Artists being artists, almost everyone involved was interested in subverting the game in some way: actively looking to use different materials, creating elaborate sub-sets of rules, or ignoring any implorations to not peek. Thus, normal game dynamics were altered and collaboration on borders and edges became paramount, a very different arrangement than that

possible with the small-scale folded-paper version. Also, unlike the traditional version, this one operated in three dimensions as a spatial entity to move through, complicating any simple schematic ideas and making any total, all-at-once viewing of the finished work impossible. Instead, as one moved through Scrawl one encountered an ever-shifting visual landscape with various artists' work colliding and intersecting at any given moment Instead of being unconsidered edges, fizzling off into blankness, the segues and the spaces between one thing and another were the site of the real action, an adventurous and surprising call-and-response from one artist to another.

For visitors, Scrawl offered a chance to view working processes as they unfolded in real time, which encouraged repeat visits and a sense of active engagement with the artists and space. The drawing became event and theatre. There was personal growth and experimentation for the artists, but also something really rich and varied for the visitor to experience. Scrawl pushed collusion between the public and the private. The project was at once collaborative and allowed for individual investment in the work. Artists tended to be generous with their working time and very involved in their own acreage and therefore often unaware of the true nature of everything going on around them. This part worked really well, even if the screening-off was a bit haphazard.

There were even a few upsets which brought people closer and provided good

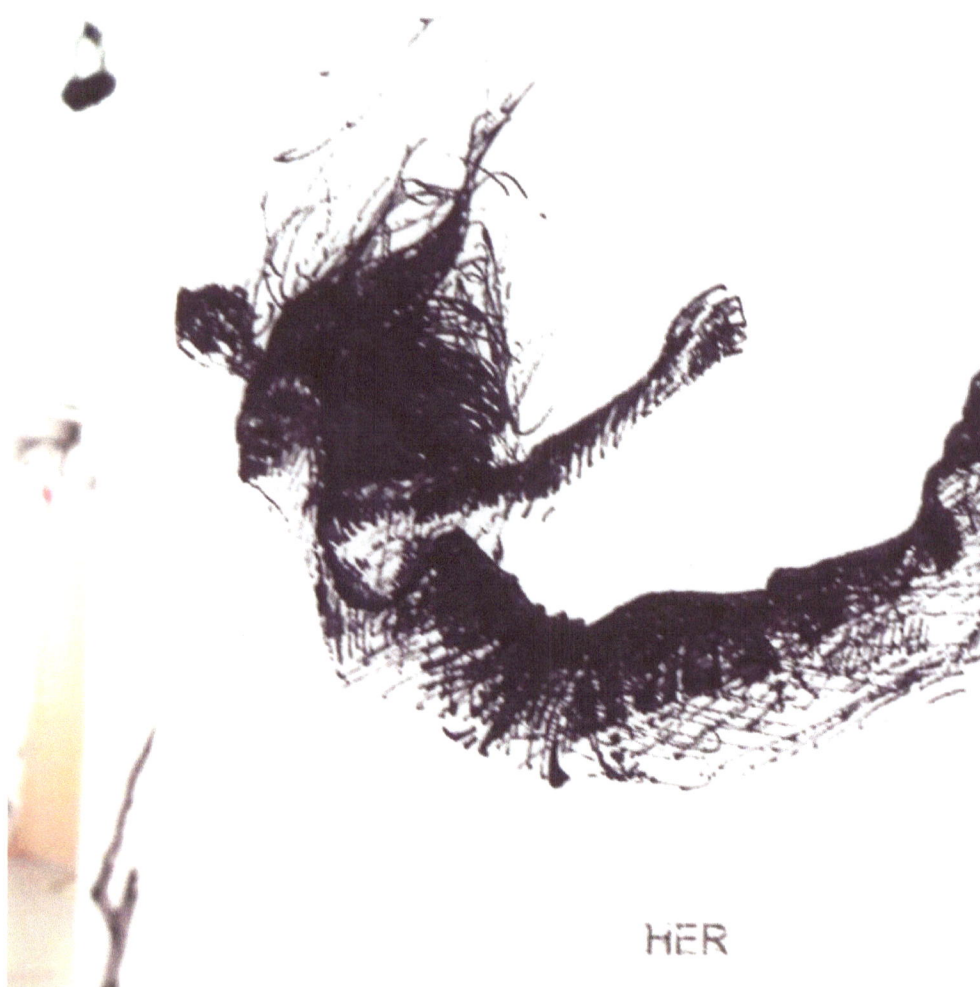

HER

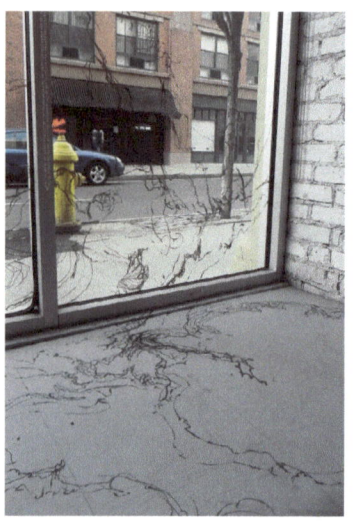

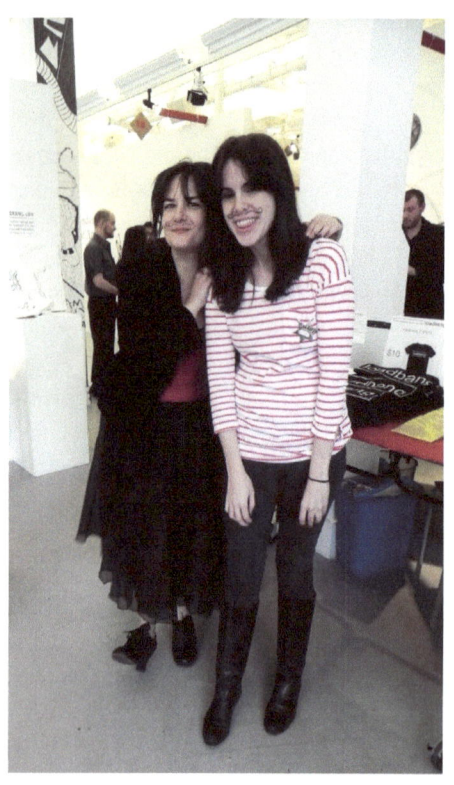

material for stories afterwards: the intern who got stuck in the supply closet, or the time a washing machine overflowed upstairs, causing a ceiling leak with streams of water pouring into the main gallery. Maegen McElderry writes of this last incident:

"We were like a bunch of roombas instinctively attacking this would-be catastrophe; were it not for the few people who were there, it could have been a disaster…" Maegen, Francis Cooke, the Sausage Crew, Caleb Hendricks and other Artspace interns all came to the rescue, averting catastrophe and converting it to the stuff of legends.

Scrawl had multiple satellite projects, We cultivated partnerships with amazing people and institutions, most notably The Aldrich Contemporary Art Museum, whose annual Draw On! event Scrawl became part of. We collaborated with The Aldrich's interim education director, Suzanne Enser-Ryan, who sent us two elegant exquisite corpse flip-books for the public to draw in, which went on to be displayed at the Museum. The public were invited to work on this in the front gallery during all of our opening hours. The Aldrich also generously arranged for artist James Esber to work on one of his participatory Osama bin Laden drawing projects in our galleries for an afternoon. We were helped by the Eli Whitney Museum, who made our huge screens as a part of a woodworking project for kids—such generous exchanges made a truly giant project like Scrawl feasible and enjoyable.

Other projects were SCRAWL-TV, a selection of short animated drawings by an international roster of artists, viewable continuously on a monitor in the front gallery. This was visible from the street or one could pull up an armchair and headphones for a more intense session. We hosted PubSCRAWL, an informal meet-up on Tuesday evenings at Artspace's Ninth Square neighbor, Firehouse 12. Artists gathered informally to draw together, had a drink, and recorded the vibe of the bar. On February 19, yoginis from Artspace's neighbor across the street, Fresh Yoga, kindly led a free class in the gallery, offering a unique drawing opportunity to capture participants as they shifted from pose to pose. We called this Stretching & SCRAWLing. The event was a challenge to both artists and yogini alike.

Towards the rear of the gallery, we installed a large-scale chalkboard wall for visitors

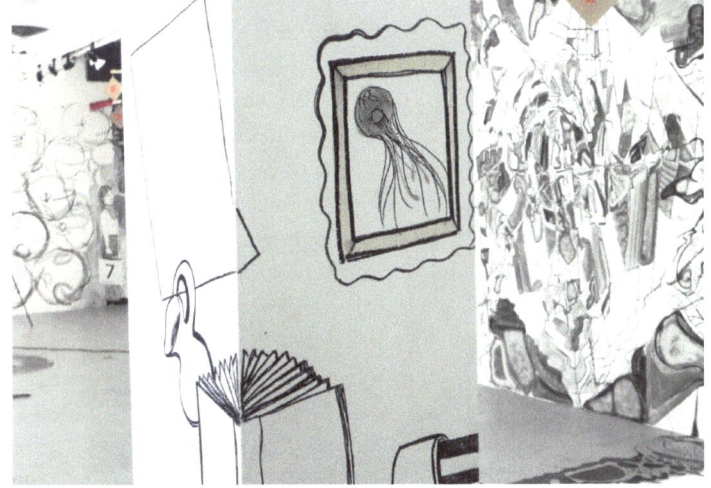

to experience "embodied drawing" for themselves. This was left until it got too clogged with imagery and then cleaned ready to start afresh. An unpredictable visual element in Scrawl, it was widely used by all. Lastly, to keep a diarist's record, we started the SCRAWLog, a book where artists and visitors could record their thoughts on Scrawl, draw, and add ideas.

All good things must come to an end, and we chose to give our exquisite corpse a festive wake to celebrate. For "The Big Reveal," the red curtain panels were all rolled up, the screens put away, and the work was unveiled. At last visible in its entirety, it flowed from one gallery to another to be publicly witnessed. The blue surgical booties were discarded, and shoes were once again visible in the space. The party celebrated the work before it was painted over the following week. Like all ephemeral events, this was bittersweet; it was marvelous because it was not going to last long.

We opened up the space and made the most of the remaining hours: we had a musical exquisite corpse by the experimental chamber group Load Bang (featuring a digitally fed head singing on a screen), special red cocktails, a cocktail napkin drawing wall, and surreal fake mustaches.

There were moments that were aggravating, stressful, worrisome, difficult; all of that has faded to the background, and what remains is what a charged and energetic force Scrawl became because of its artists. After the exhibition ended and we painted the gallery white, Artspace seemed so quiet, faded, and mute by comparison.

It felt sad and a bit staid, except that the place still echoes with the visual ghosts of Scrawl. When I walk through the galleries I don't see a plain white column, I see Anna's spindly tower spanning its height; I still see the Sausage Crew's totem pole with clever use of the electrical sockets; I see the Futurists' ants parading across the floor, Jean's magic beads, Vito's rows of toilet bowls…

This catalogue is its marker.
Martha Lewis
Scrawl Exhibition Organizer
July 2011 ■

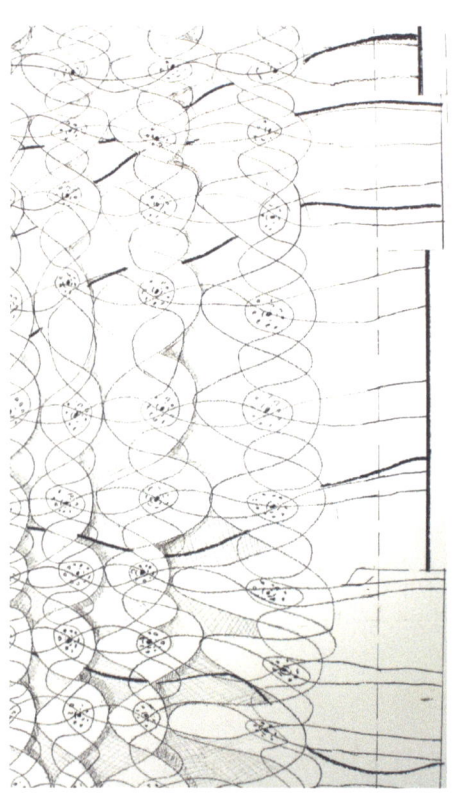

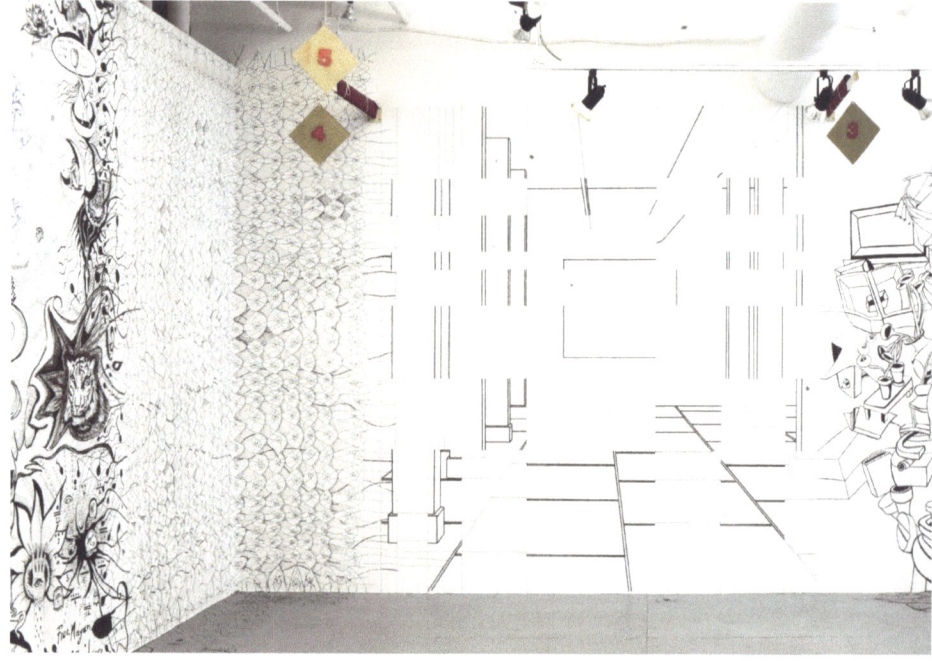

Cat Balco

Cat Balco's work, inspired by the spirituality, patterns, and gestural involvement of the body inherent in ancient art forms, seemed a natural fit given Scrawl's precept of embodied drawing. Her art has a light, effortless quality to it, which appears spontaneous, flowing and casual. This is, of course, the result of years of practice and a honed vision of her work as a holistic practice.

Her drawing for Scrawl invoked a textile, with interwoven strands moving across from Francis Cooke's broken geometric interior to flow around a corner and into Andres Madariaga's complex evocation of birth, with her rippling strands morphing sinuously into spreading spermatozoa.

In terms of this interaction, Balco writes: "It was easy for me to imagine how to link my piece to those next to it because my work resembles a weaving. I simply imagined I was knitting or tying it to the works next door. I did think it looked a lot better when I made some long, bolder lines that connected the two pieces adjacent to mine to each other—not just to mine—THROUGH my piece."

Much of Balco's practice rests squarely in the realm of painting, with marks and lines being wide and brushy, with a real emphasis on color to create depth. With the Sharpie, the marks were by nature very different and of course texture had to replace color as a means of creating spatial difference. She segued into the new materials with seeming ease.

Balco writes of her experience: "I've never worked on a large piece in Sharpie before. Doing so opened up some new possibilities. I also haven't thought about drawing in a long time … and it was exciting to work with graphic media again. I've made a number of drawings since and the Sharpie marker has become a studio staple."

Cat Balco received her MFA in Painting in 2007 from the Yale School of Art, where she was the recipient of the Helen Winternitz Award in Painting and the Gloucester Landscape Painting Prize. She has been awarded residency fellowships through the Weir Farm Trust, the Albers Foundation, the Vermont Studio Center, and the Yale School of Art at Norfolk. Balco's work has been exhibited throughout the northeast; her paintings have been discussed in international publications including ArtInfo.com, *The New York Times*, and the London-based magazine *Bon International*. Recently, she received a public commission for the lobby of the new 360 State Street building in New Haven. She is currently assistant professor of painting and drawing at Hartford Art School, University of Hartford. ■

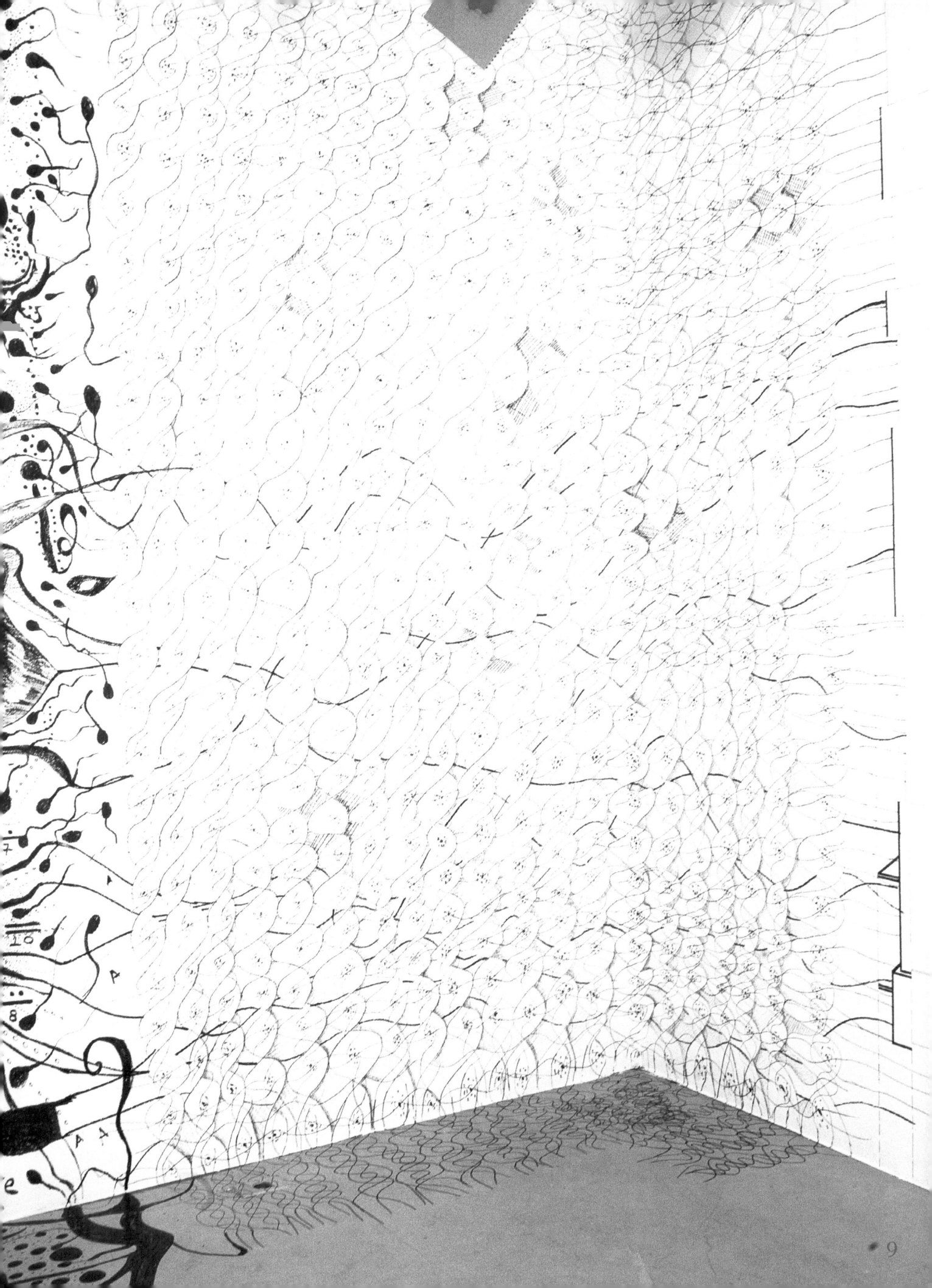

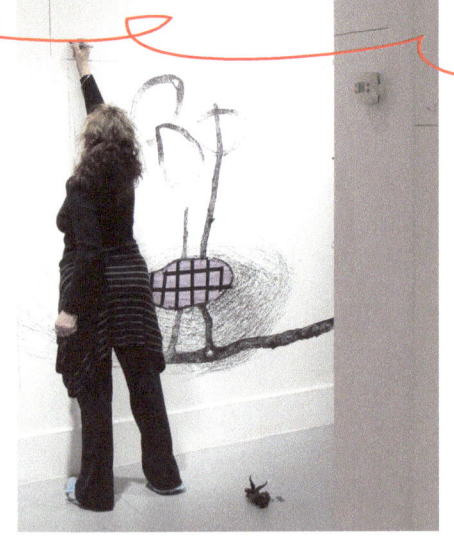

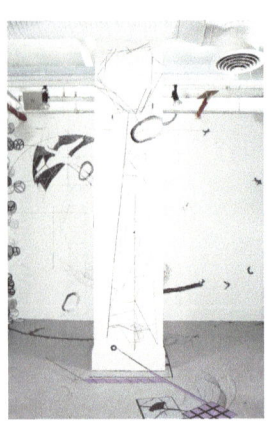

Anna Broell Bresnick

Anna Broell Bresnick is one of Scrawl's most experienced artists. This was reflected in the decisive way she approached her space and her generosity with input to the other artists around her.

She writes of her time during Scrawl: "It created excitement, pressure, competition and a small amount of anxiety in the beginning—all stuff that is pretty energizing …The main difference for me was that the "drawing" now became a "three-dimensional drawing" or "walk-through drawing" never to be seen as a whole. The viewer, once entering the space, was continuously introduced to new combinations of images including aspects of the adjoining drawing of other artists on the right and left. This entire concept was very different than my studio work (drawing and sculpture as two separate issues), and introduced exciting possibilities for future explorations and projects. "…The adherence to the limitation of materials forces you out of a comfort zone which is really important from time to time ... I feel enough confidence in my studio work to allow myself the freedom of exploring a few new avenues through the use of materials and processes I might feel uncomfortable with. The anxiety comes from having to do this publicly, but I felt willing, challenged and actually excited to try this thing out. The exclusive use of pens allowed me to experiment with using a drill (with a pen insert) as a drawing tool.

"…The collaborative process then began as I approached the edges of the drawing. I was somewhat surprised to find out how complicated (difficult to solve) some of those collaborative edges were as well as how fluid some others became…the process of working from the center out, and then trying to become collaborative at the edge of each side of the drawing was a great experience as well as a challenge. …I loved the combination of the three of us (my neighbors and myself). As you walked through the space, the entire piece started with intense density on the left and worked its way into extreme scarcity on the right.

"… Once the entire project was revealed, it proved to be a very dynamic, exciting environment. Last, but not least, this project generated a great audience both during the time of its creation as well as at the reception (The Big Reveal), which was great, and really well attended."

Anna Broell Bresnick studied at the Akademie fuer Angewante Kunst in Vienna, Austria, and received her MFA from San Jose State University. She has exhibited in galleries throughout the United States as well as in Berlin, Rome, and Vienna. Over the last ten years, Bresnick has collaborated with dancers and musicians in the creation of installations for performances. ■

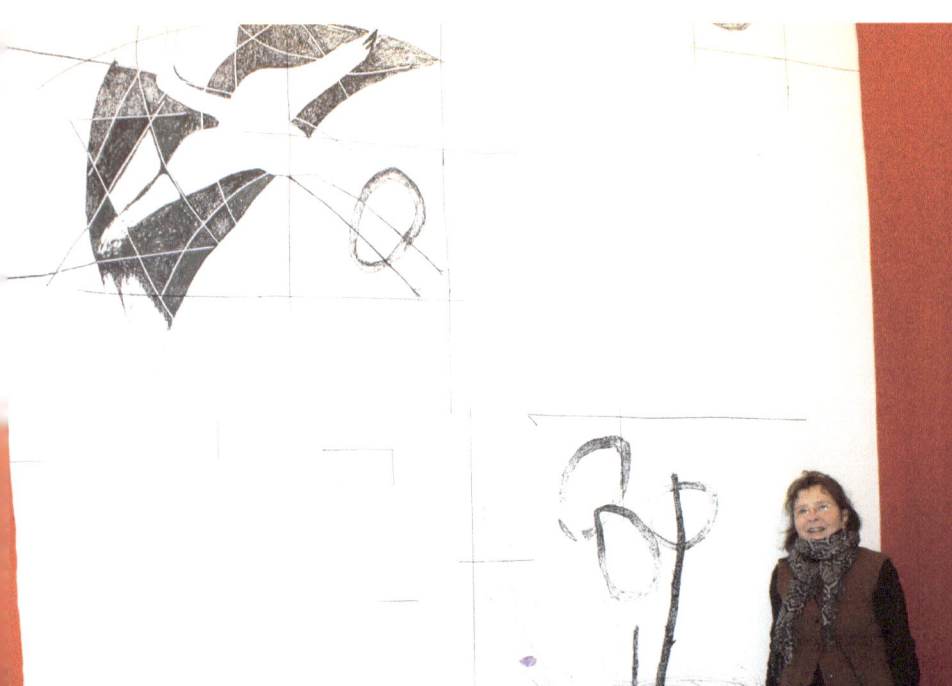

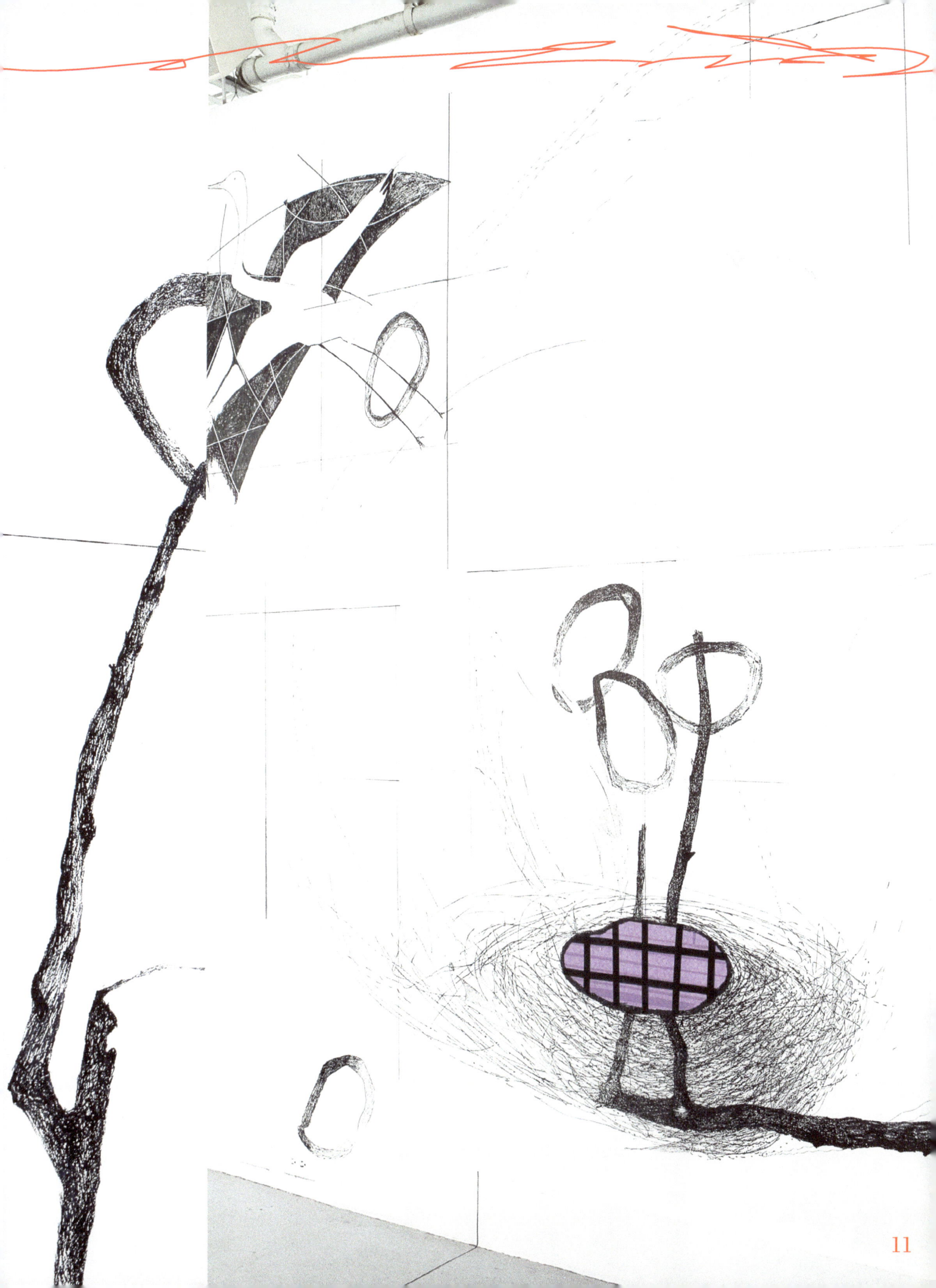

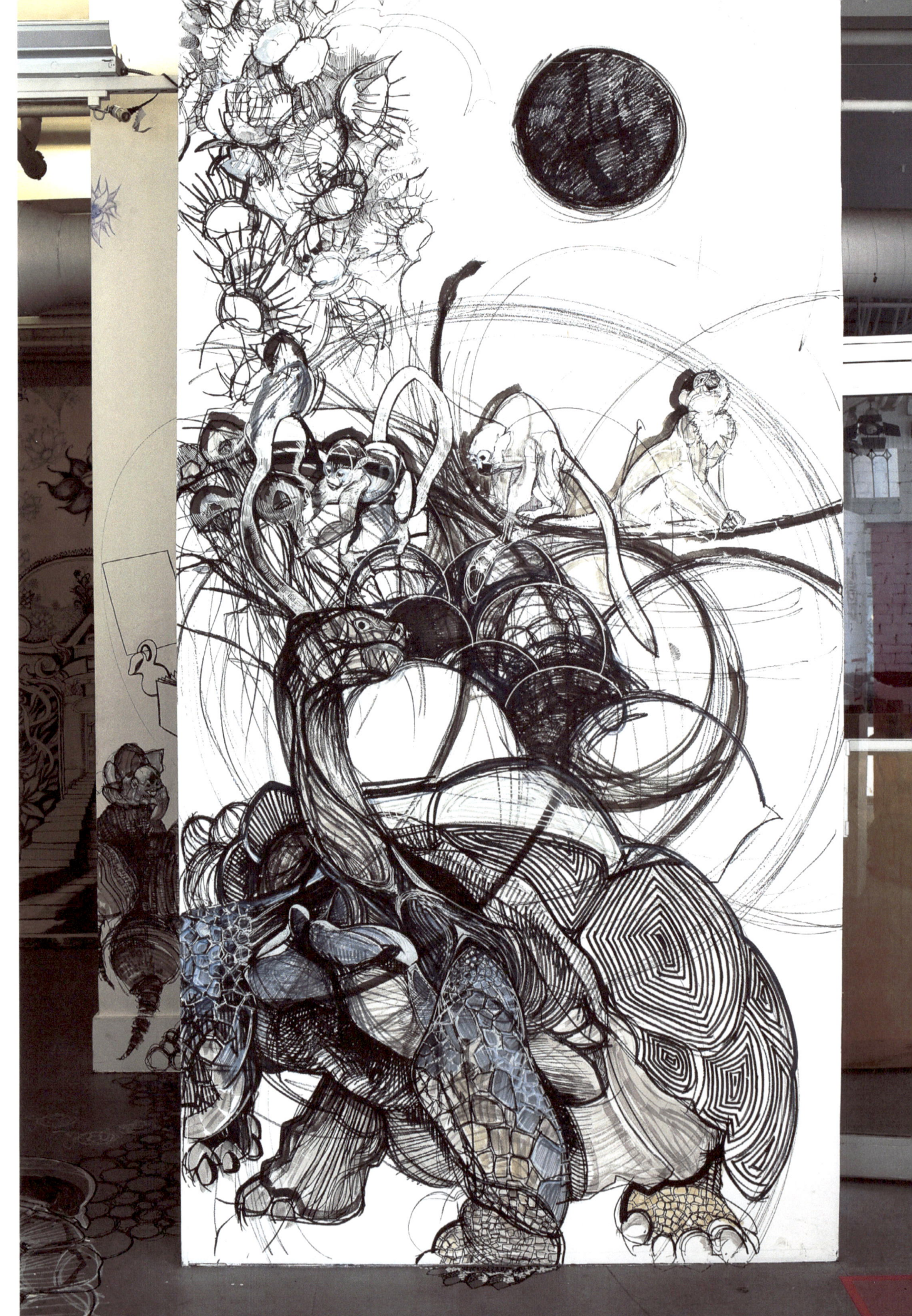

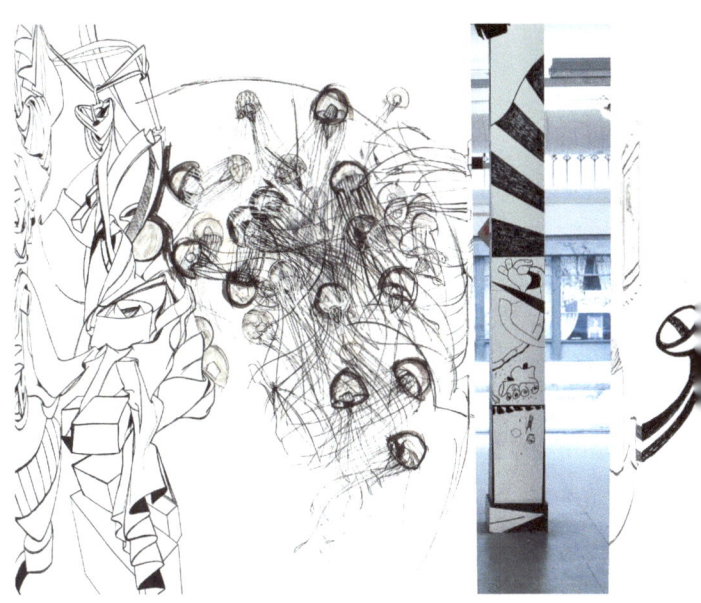

Alexis Brown

I n addition to participating in the exhibition, Alexis Brown collaborated on many other aspects of Scrawl. She helped conceive the look and modus operandi of the show, researched ideas for this catalogue, and single-handedly produced the limited edition T-shirts and posters. She also worked with students from the Betsy Ross Arts Magnet School to create their own series of exquisite corpse/ Frankenstein drawings. Prodigious is the only word to describe her.

Brown's seemingly boundless energy did not stop there: for her portion of the Scrawl space she created a flourishing world of animals, a bestiary of diverse origins which thrived and spread over walls, floor, and columns. Much of Alexis's practice involves accurately depicting animals in a style that is at once gestural and bold, while containing an anatomist's concern for accuracy. Her work for Scrawl epitomized this and gave her space to run rampant with her predilection for life-size imagery. Her world of abundance and plenty are tinged with the pathos inherent in reflecting a place that no longer exists. It holds the sadness of species extinction and the active fight for native habitats and daily survival due to human encroachment.

For those that remain, Brown's vivid marks make their virtual liveliness all the more poignant, without tipping over the edge of sentimentality. Her oeuvre's nostalgia for

a place of abundance retains the violence and sacrifice inherent in the Darwinian order of things.

During Scrawl she magnificently collaborated directly with Laura Watt and Rashmi Talpade to occupy a teeming corner of the gallery that was painful to paint over in the end. Sea turtles melted into abstract hexagonal lozenges, animals perched around off-kilter picture frames and dissolved into floor bubbles. The unlikeliest of the pairings was the best part—a tit-for-tat response to each other's offerings that swirled and eddied in a giddy flow of marks and edges.

Alexis Brown received her BFA from the School of the Arts Institute, Chicago. She currently teaches printmaking at the Creative Arts Workshop, and works with high school students in an environmental stewardship program at the Eli Whitney Museum, both in New Haven, CT. Brown's practice combines printmaking, drawing, and animal illustration to make vivid large-scale works which combine strong gesture with anatomical accuracy. A native of New Haven, she has exhibited her work throughout the northeast ■

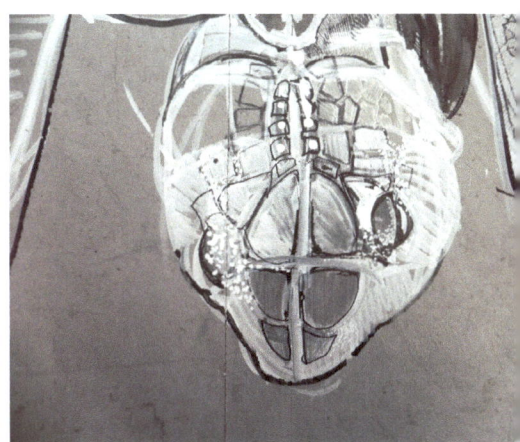

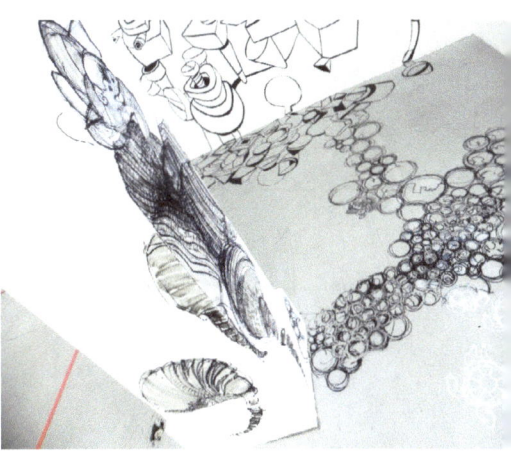

13

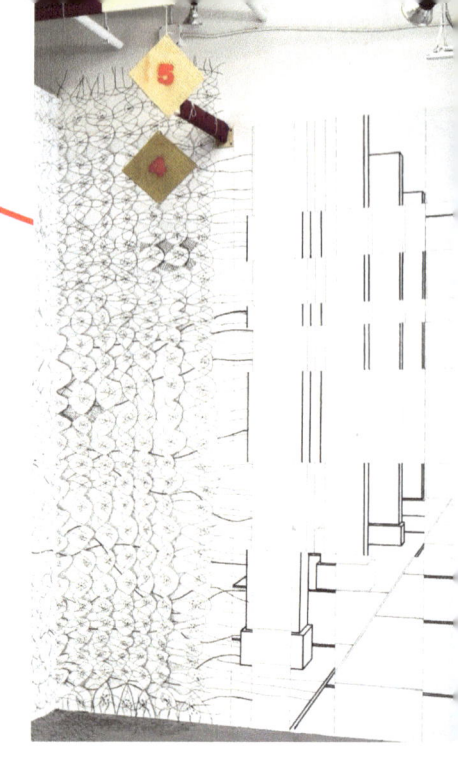

F rancis W. Cooke is a practicing architect and an accomplished draftsman, as was reflected in his piece for Scrawl which is precise, spatial, and planned out in advance. He worked in an organized thoughtful way, adhering to the rules of the game at every turn, and good-naturedly dealing with the spanners that inevitably flew into the works—such as the gallery's ceiling suddenly leaking buckets of water one evening. Despite such misadventures, his experience with Scrawl was positive:

"Working at this scale was an astounding experience. It began to bridge the spatial projection and spatial experience divide inherent in architecture. I loved the challenge of drawing big. It forced me to organize the picture plane effectively so I could work at the scale of my body. This organizational requirement allowed me to work through an issue with proportion that had been bedeviling me for some time. I also enjoyed the materiality of drawing on an over-painted wall. The texture of the wall greatly diminished the quality of line I could produce and it took me in different directions. I learned from it."

In terms of the rules and materials: "Limitations are my breakfast, lunch and dinner. I don't do well without them; I am nourished and inspired by them. The desire to augment my work with respect to the other work that was visible was nearly overwhelming. . . . I did however resist.

"The exquisite corpse is intended to not be collective; it was only so in this case by accident and schedule. That actually made it nice. As it turned out, my neighbor to the left, Cat Balco, had a change in her schedule and we were working together on one session. We devised a connection strategy. The neighbor on the right, Rashmi Talpade, followed on without any conversation in exactly the same manner.

"The process of the whole was interesting to witness (some planned, some winged it, some worked weeks, others hours), the outcome was grand and shockingly coherent."

Francis W. Cooke

Cooke considers drawing to be fundamental to his approach to design. He finds drawing to have immense value as a tool with which one can explore, express and explicate truths; seeing beyond the "real" to find meaning within abstractions. He received his B.Arch from Oklahoma State University and his M.Arch from the University of Pennsylvania. ■

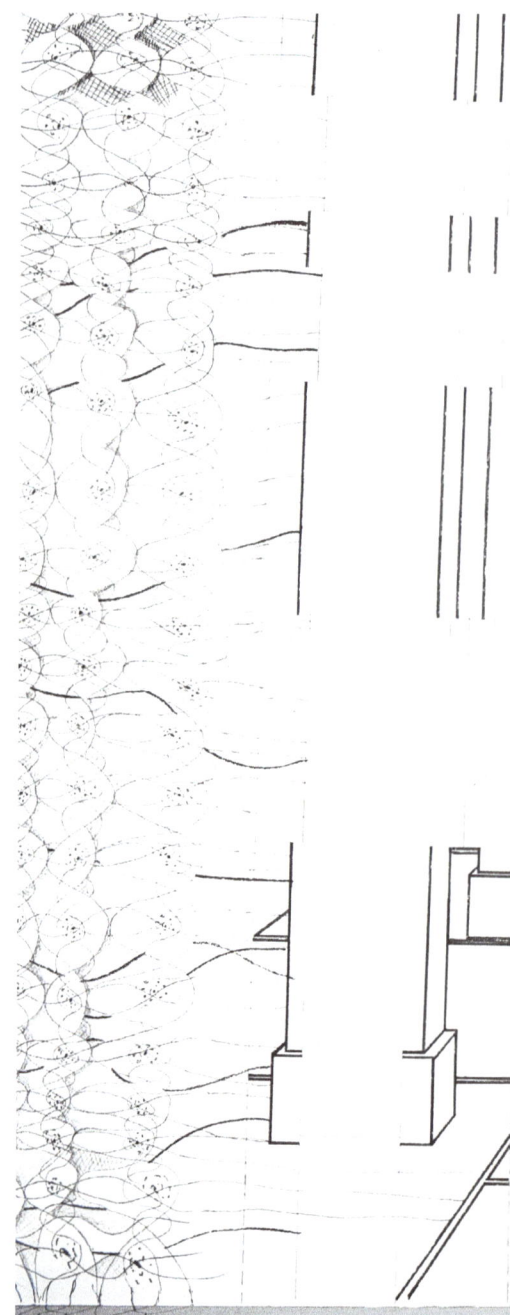

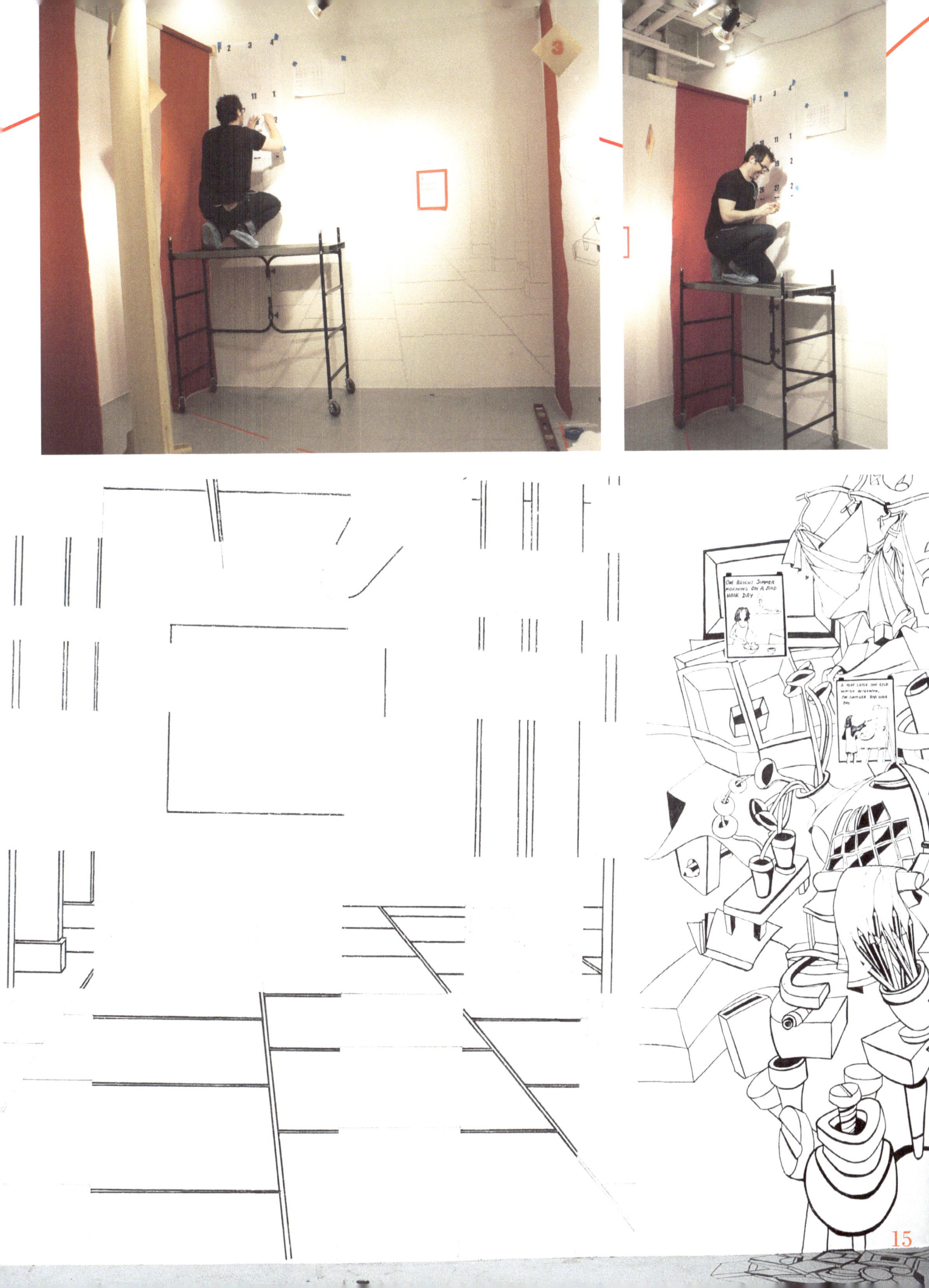

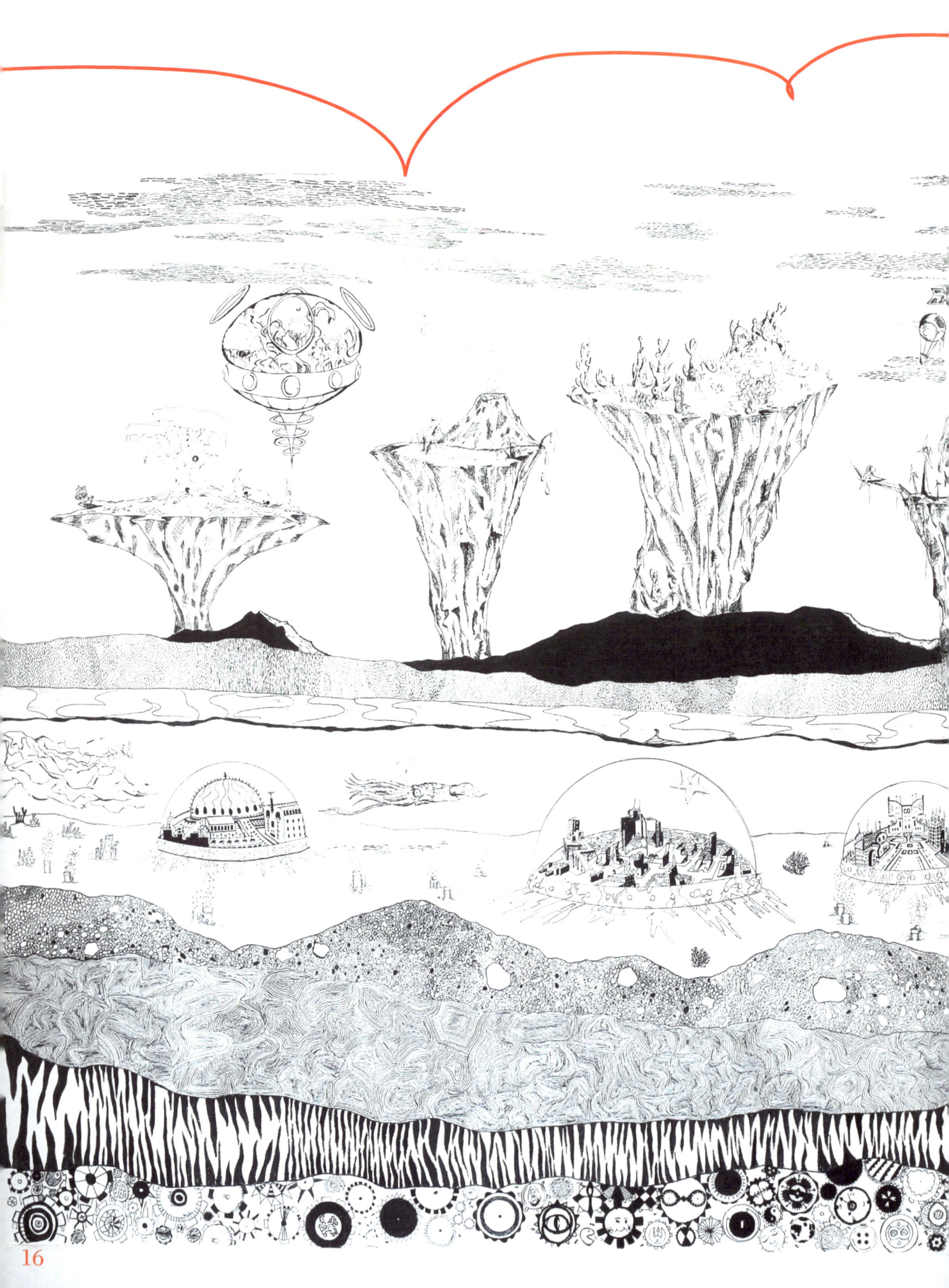

The Futurists

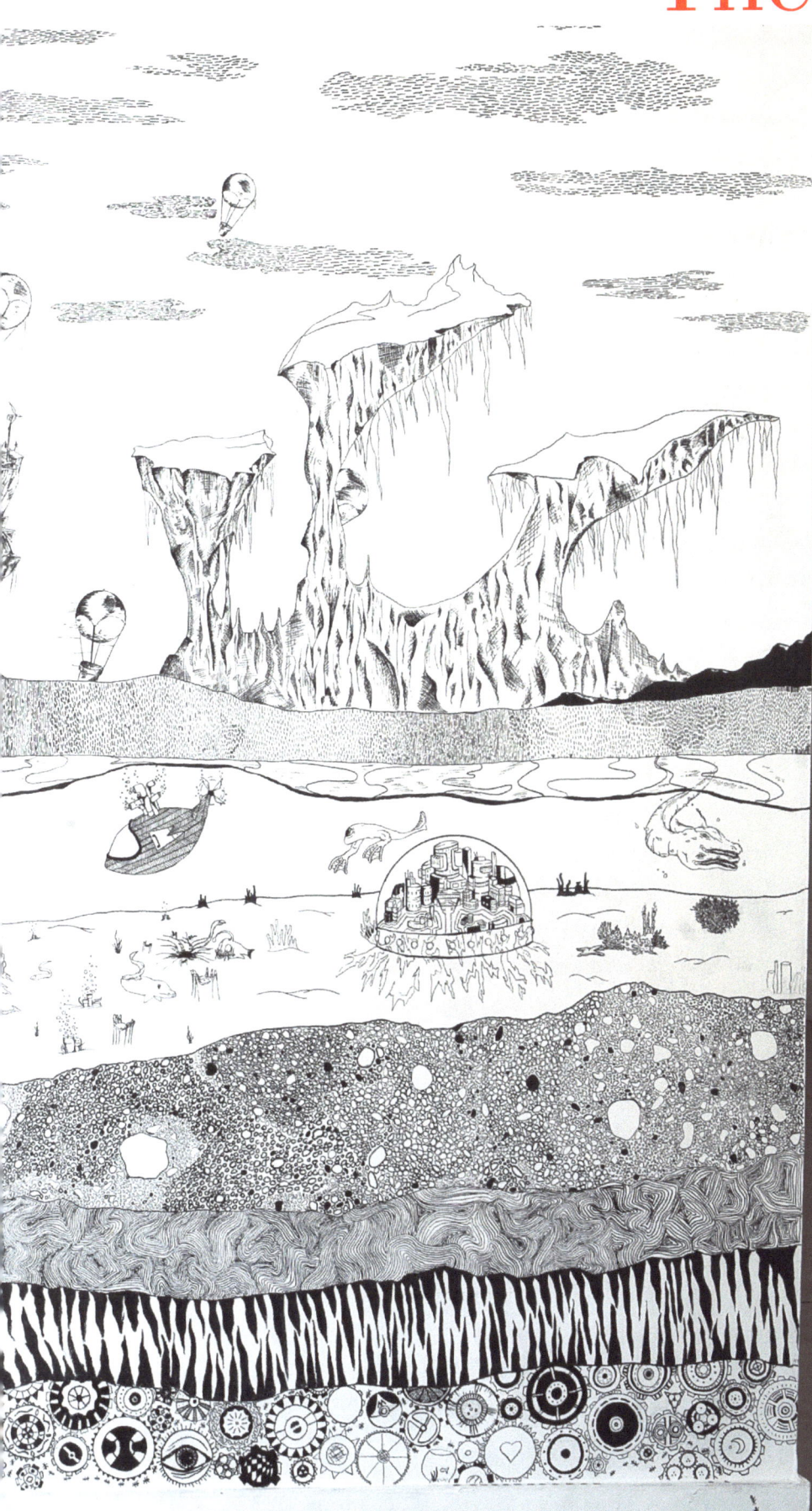

Karen Dow and her class of drawing students from the Educational Center for the Arts:
Ashley Babson,
Diana Carter,
Max Coleman,
Stacy Friedman,
Lia Hodson,
Rebecca Mills,
Je'Nae Pelletier,
Danielle Pereira,
Ariel Pond,
Alexander Sorenson,
Aja Suarez,
Angela Yang

The Futurists team collaborated to create a work related to ideas of "utopia."

Dow writes of their experience:

"Our preliminary process as a team was to doodle as we watched two films: *Blade Runner* and *Metropolis*. We discussed the themes in the films and reacted to the imagery that stood out for us. It grew from there. We were pleased with the result and felt like it exceeded our expectations.

"I was pleasantly surprised that my students handled making a public work so well. We had very specific times that we could work on the piece. It was fun trying to navigate twelve high school students working at once. They worked side by side literally for three hours at a stretch.

"I like parameters. I like the challenge of trying to make such a 'bare bones'

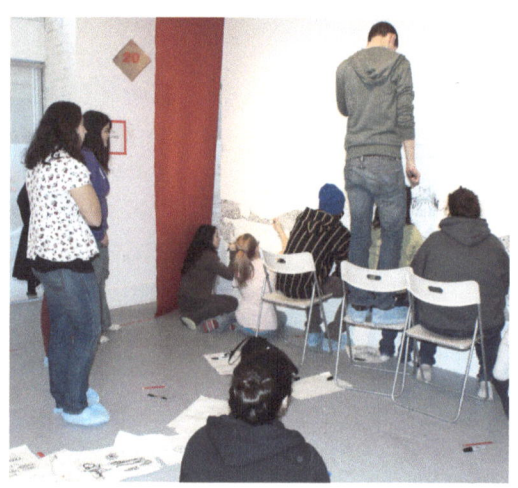 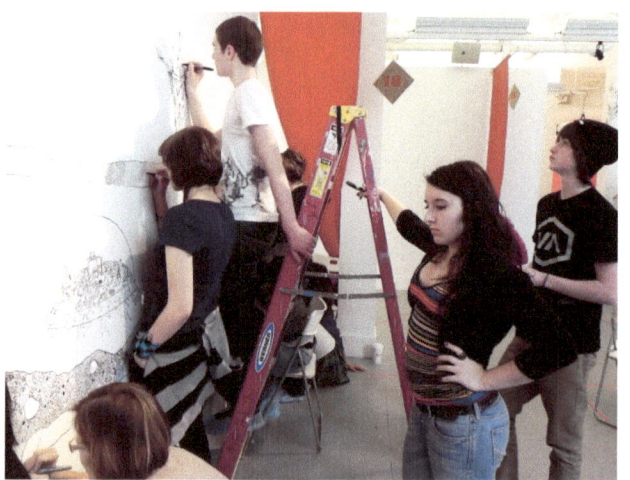

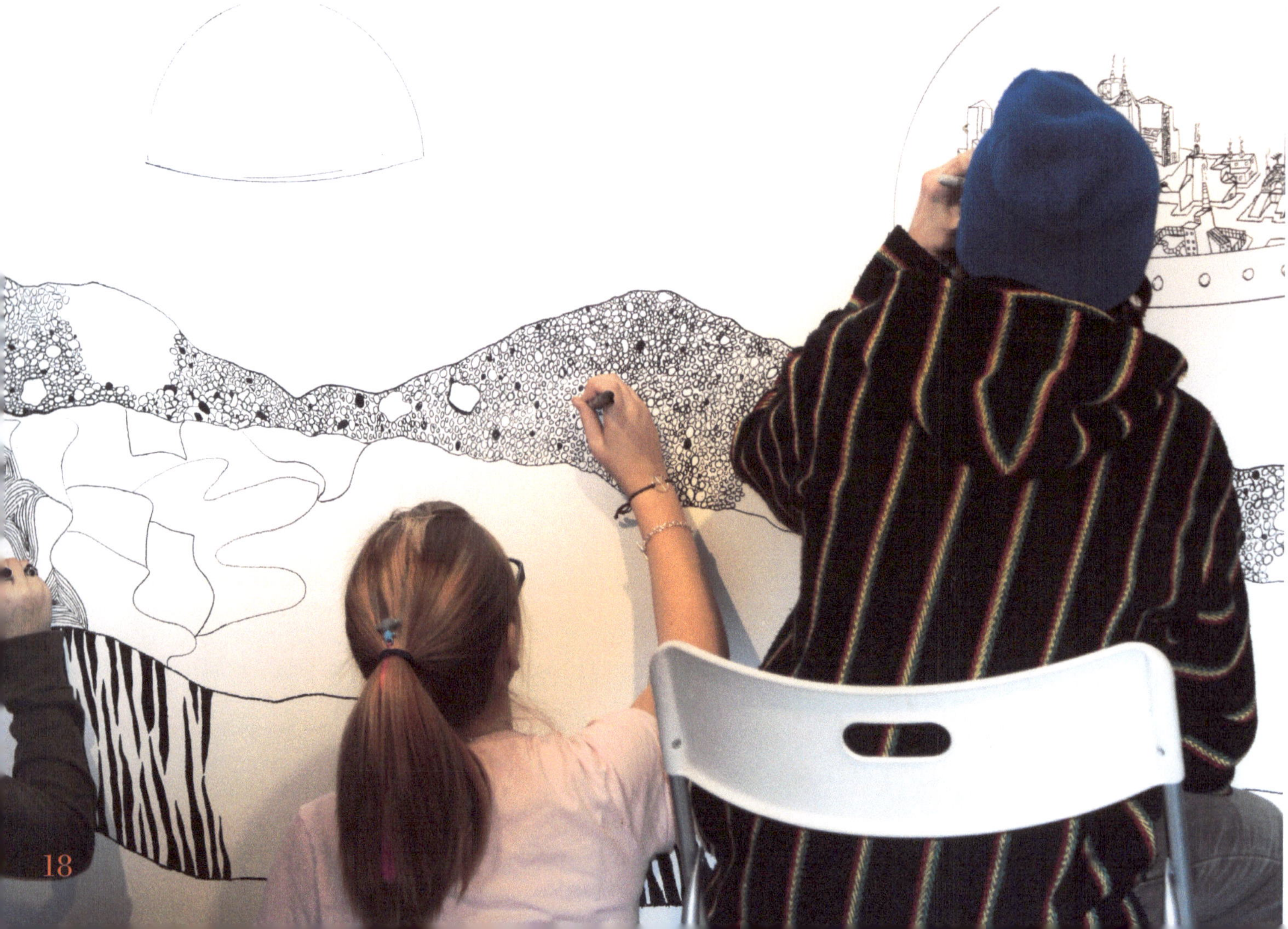

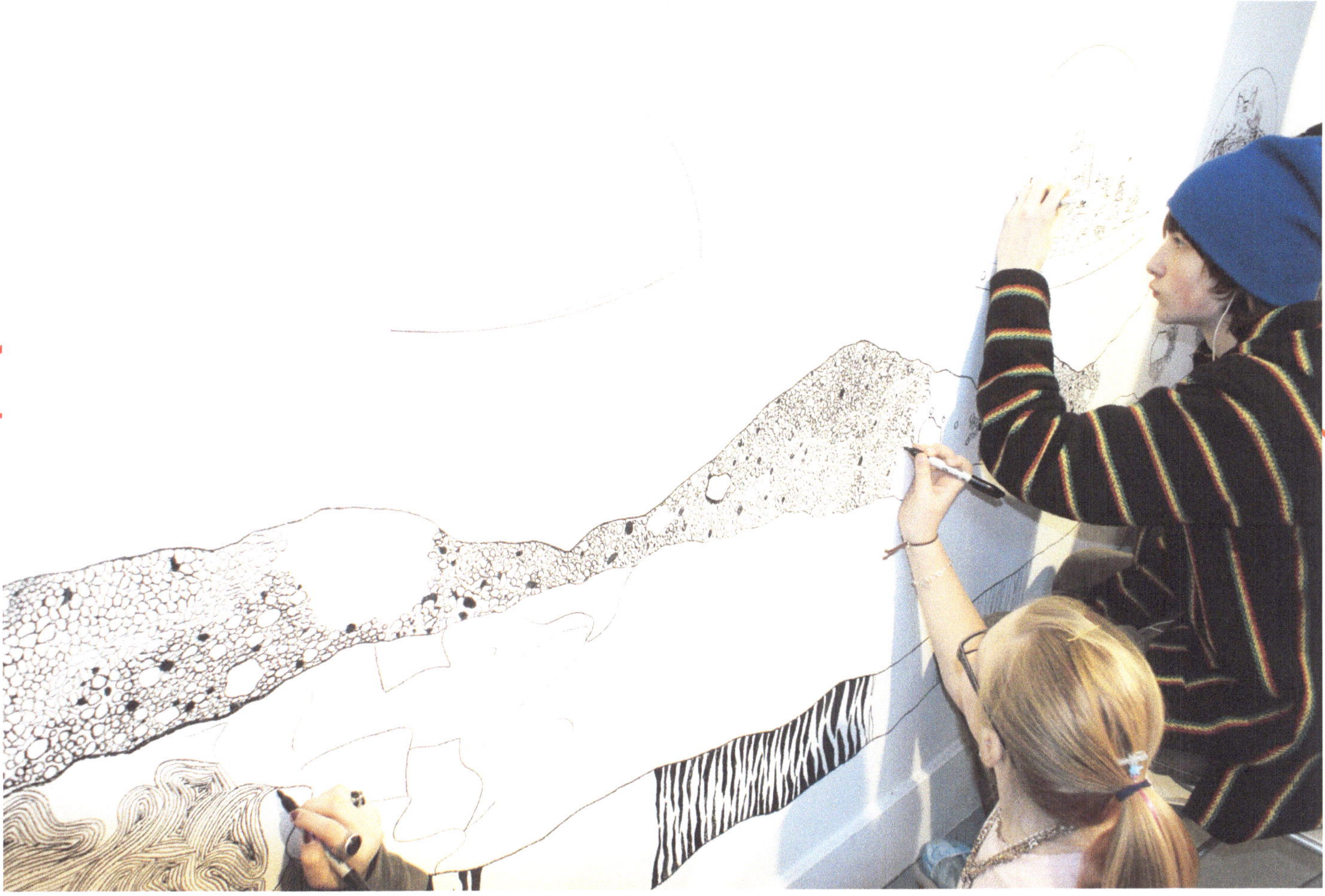

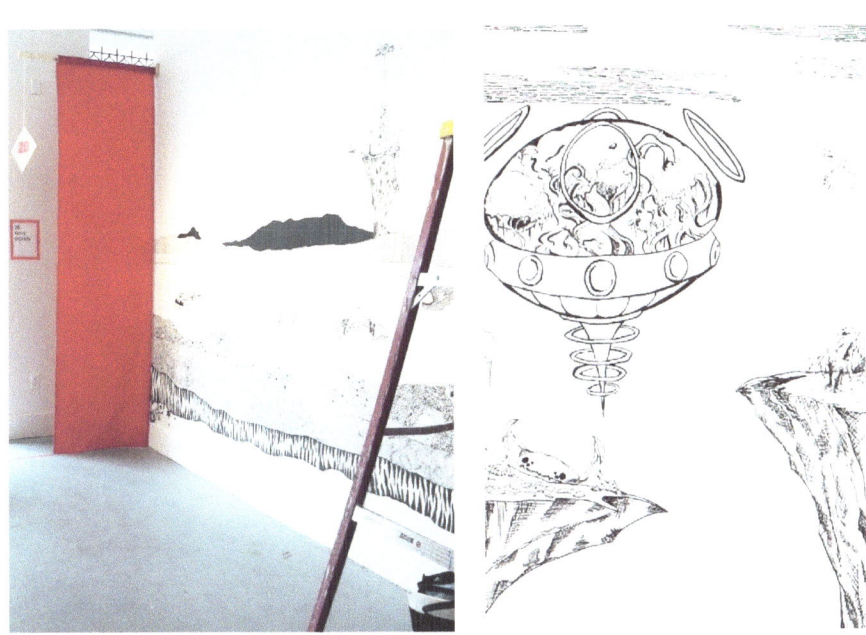

project unique and unified at the same time. I think you can get a real sense of individual expression when the materials are limited.

"I loved the work environment. It was exciting and stimulating to be part of such a large project. Part of our group's 'ornatenesss' was due to the fact that we had twelve people working at once on a single wall. I think it gave us a spectacular result. We were only aware that the piece looked the way we wanted it to."

Futurist leader and artist Karen Dow received her MFA in Painting from the Yale School of Art. She is the recipient of numerous awards, including the Joan Mitchell Foundation Career Enhancement Grant, and has exhibited her work in New England, New York, and Germany. Her students are from the ECA, a high school with a dedicated focus on the arts, and have bright, promising art futures ahead of them. ◼

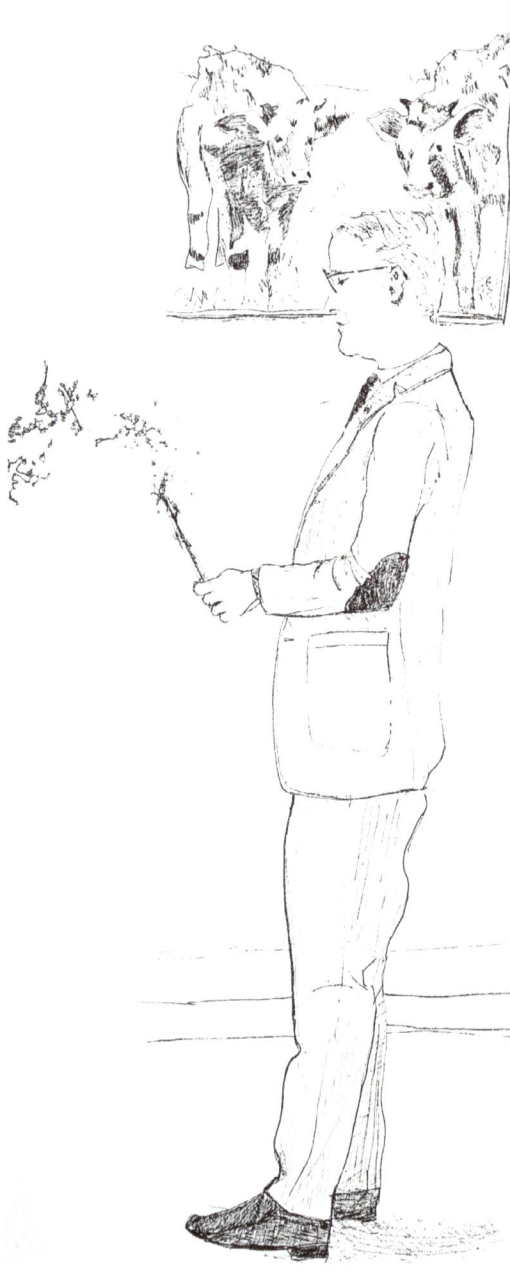

Transposing a space seen a year ago and remembered with a photograph, then superimposing it onto the walls of Artspace's gallery, Laura Gardner made her piece for Scrawl become a life-size linear souvenir, and an example of drawing's simple ability to time travel. Her scene, derived from the National Art Center in Tokyo, was populated with known and imaginary figures—including some composites of friends— wandering the galleries contemplating art. Her work was very popular with visitors, who liked to have their pictures taken with the life-sized figures.

Laura writes of her project: "… I thought it was fun and drew people in, which is what I wanted: an interesting interior with people looking back at the viewer. The other thing I really wanted to do in this piece was to convey a sense of pulling the viewer in to this space that I loved so much…I never draw in Sharpie, so that was a first. Normally I sketch in pencil and charcoal, and then either paint or go over my lines in ink, but I rarely start with a permanent line as I did in Scrawl…I liked the impact of a bold black line on the walls…The work definitely comes to life faster. Especially when I was drawing the faces of the people in the gallery, having to put it down right (or as close to right as I could get it) the first time was a good challenge for me.

"Interestingly, I started taking a scientific illustration class a few weeks before the start of Scrawl, and the instructor concentrated…on showing us how to really leverage our medium … to get an expanse of textures, tones, etc. I used some of the lessons learned— such as drawing fur on scientific specimens, or using stipple—to make my all-Sharpie drawing more vibrant…

"Working with the other artists (around) was funny… it was fun to collaborate with some of the other artists, to share ideas, etc. Some of the more exuberant teams definitely

Laura Gardner

dominated the vibe of the gallery while they worked, so there definitely was a little healthy tension, or maybe just interest in what was going on, especially when folks were laughing or playing the flute. I had several people pose for my piece, and we'd be talking or carrying on ourselves, so it may have looked like I was having a private life drawing class. What was fun was when the models came week after week to check my progress, etc., or hold the ladder while I was drawing in the skylights…At first I was wondering what it would be like to draw if there were a crowd, but there was normally just a steady trickle of visitors so that I could work and focus well but still felt some connection to the audience."

Originally trained as an art historian, Gardner received her graduate training in London, where she worked at the both the British and Leighton House Museums. Scrawl is her first exhibition in Connecticut. ■

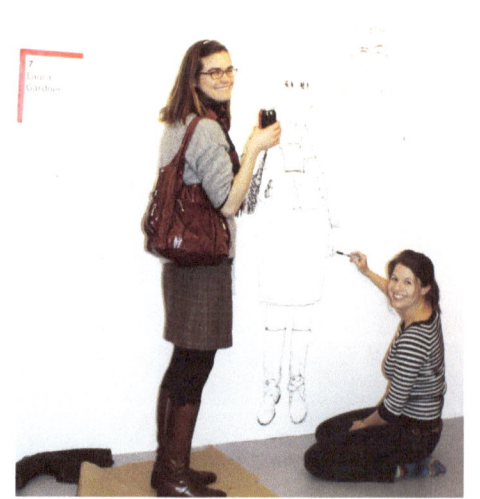

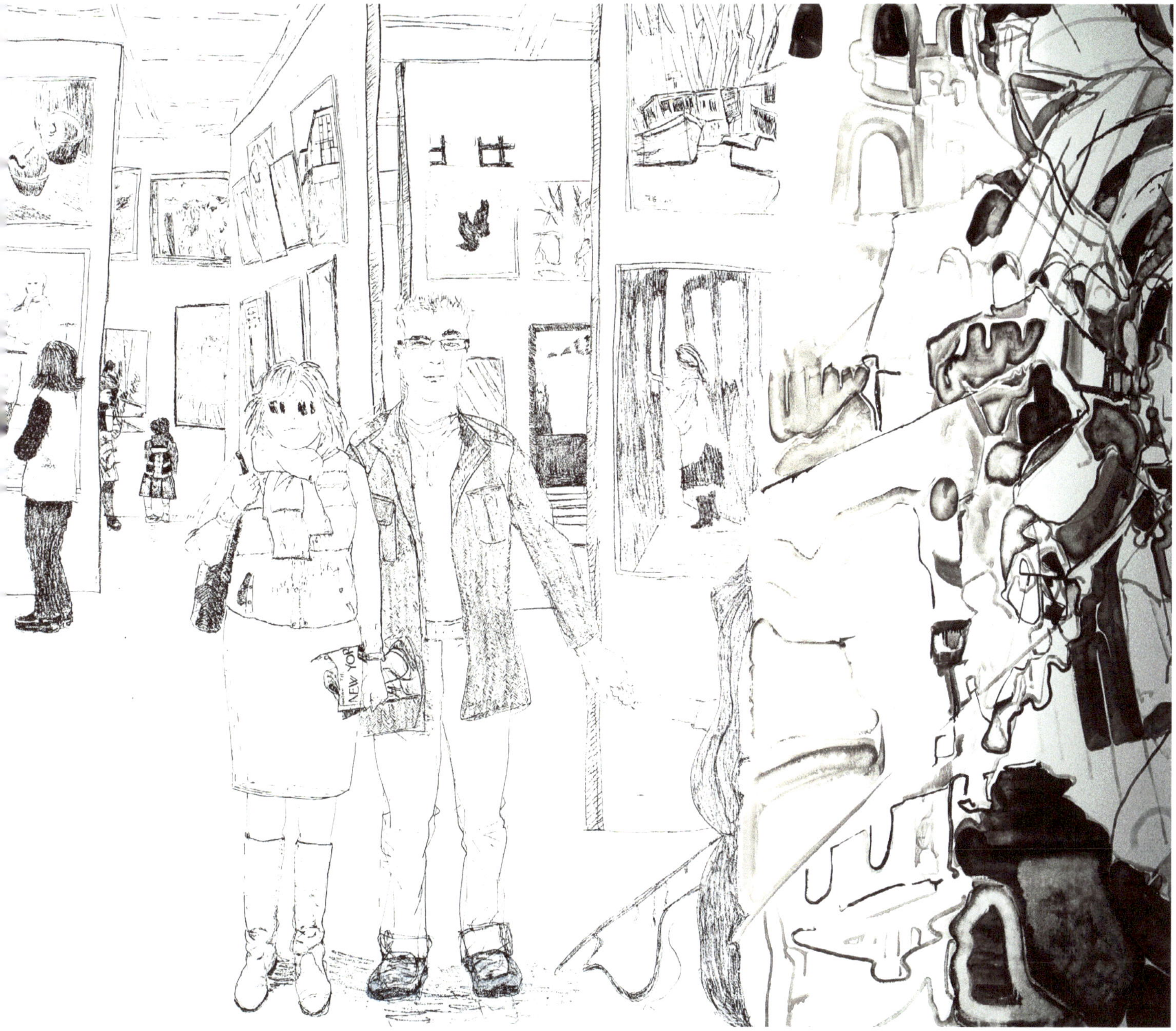

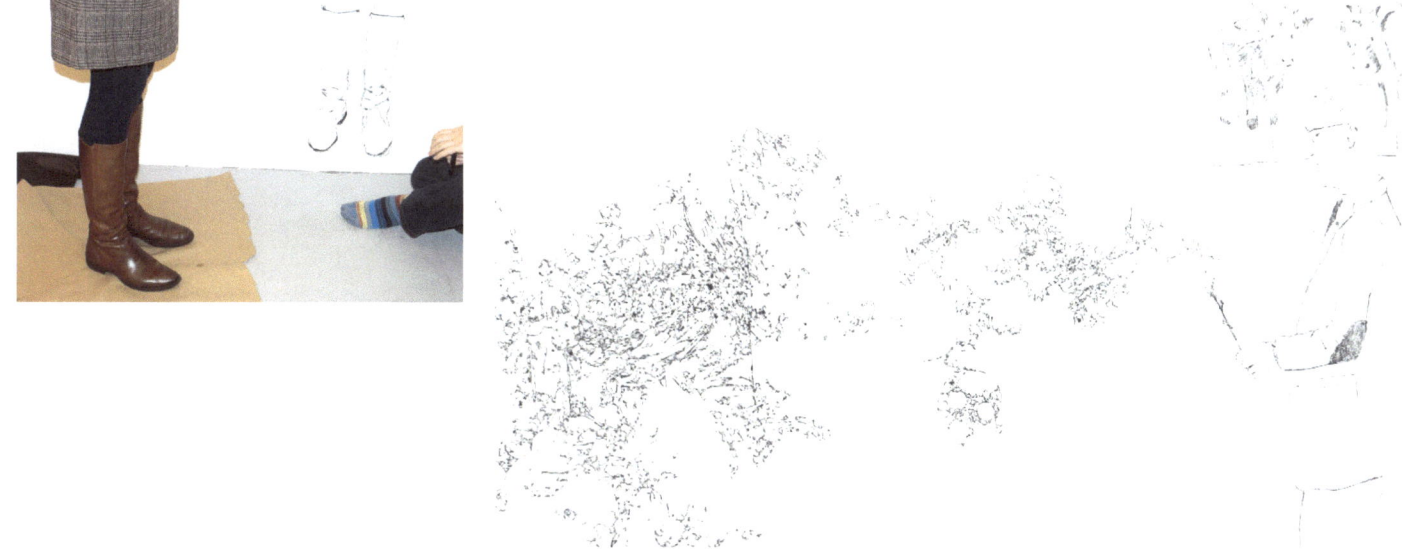

Zachary Keeting produced an exuberant zigzagging work which expanded to fill his space with bravado. The work abutted Andres Madariaga and Laura Gardner, offering an abstract pause from their pushing of the space through perspectival means. One of the pleasing aspects of Scrawl was the difference in the artists' approaches to their given work spaces. This gave the visitor an Alice-in-Wonderland-like sense of shifting mental landscapes and memories, focuses, and preferences.

Zachary writes about what made Scrawl different from his usual studio practice: "Scale mostly, and the temporary nature of the project. I'd never done a wall painting before. Linking up became tricky because of the irregular schedules and varying speeds of each participating artist. I wasn't interested in the theatrical, group element…I preferred painting alone. Keeping it pared down technically, while at the same time resisting minimal visual

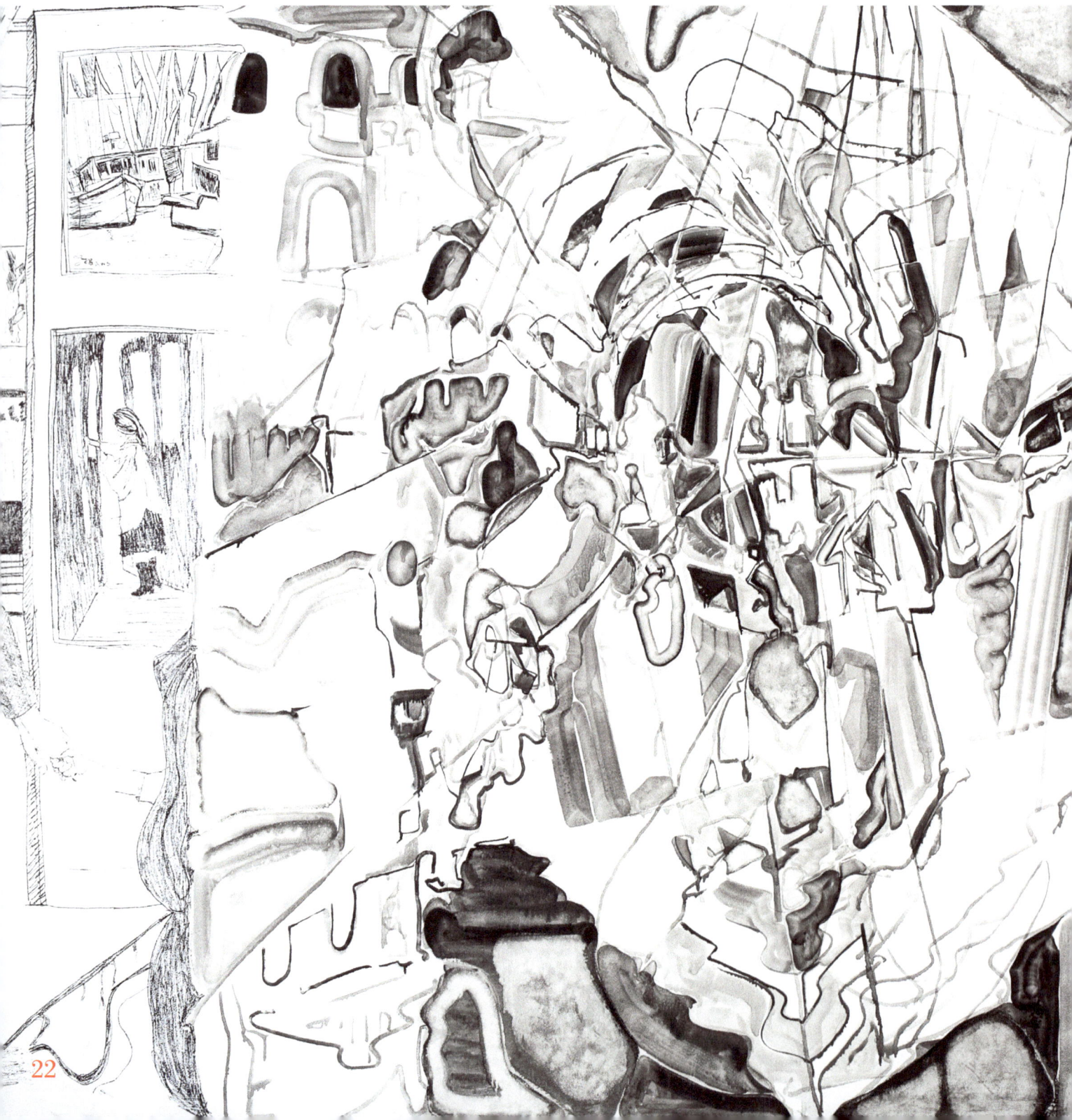

decisions was fun."

He says of Scrawl as a whole: "Strong, courageous drawing made this project worthwhile."

Zachary Keeting explores the tension between precision and abandon. His process is one of innovative improvisation, using speed and gesture to make broad expressive works. He received his MFA from Boston University, and a BFA, Summa Cum Laude, from Alfred University. Keeting has been awarded numerous residencies, including Yaddo, Byrdcliffe, and the Millay Colony. His work has been shown in numerous exhibitions throughout New England and New York, including a recent group show at Mass MoCA. He has also been a 2011 visiting artist at Hartford Art School, University of Hartford, and is currently painting instructor at ACES Educational Center for the Arts in New Haven.

With fellow artist Chris Joy, he is the co-creator of the blog *Gorky's Granddaughter*, which creates an expanding video archive of artists discussing their work from their studios. ■

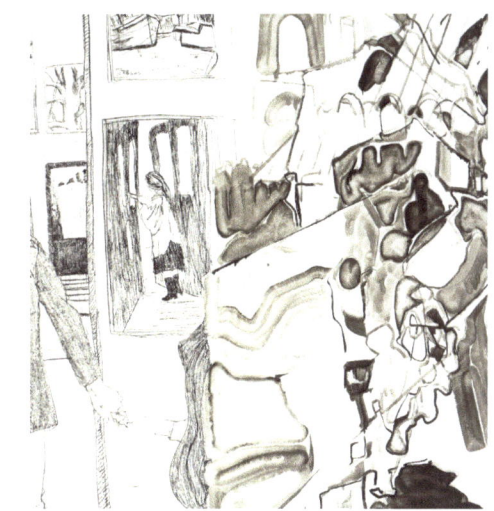

Zachary Keeting

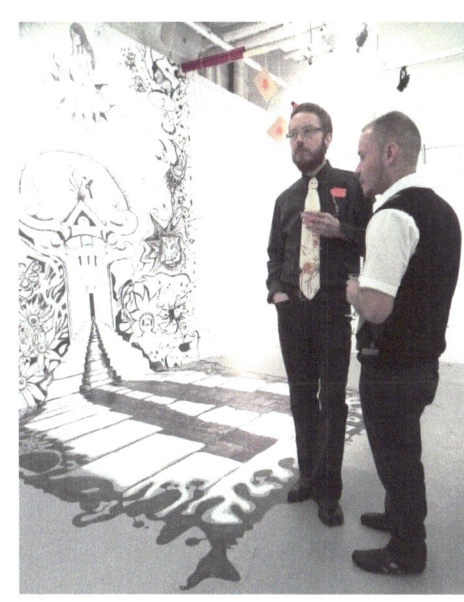

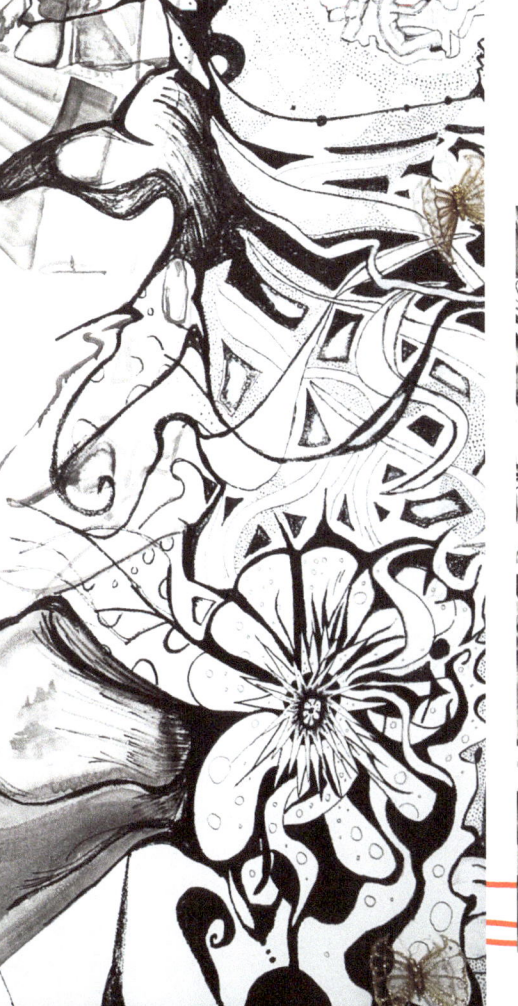

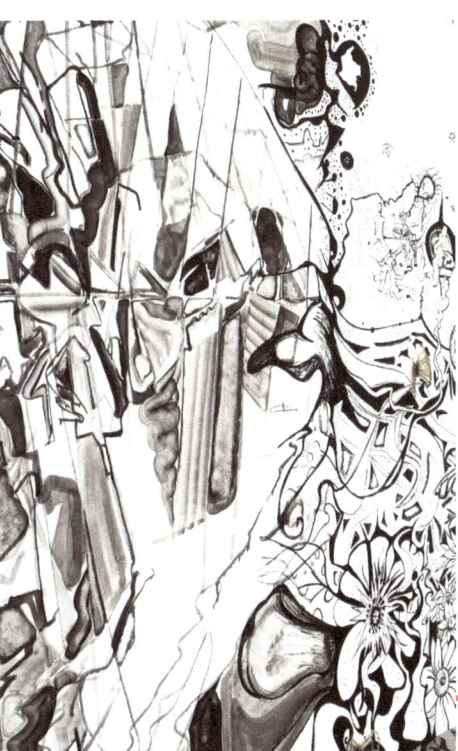

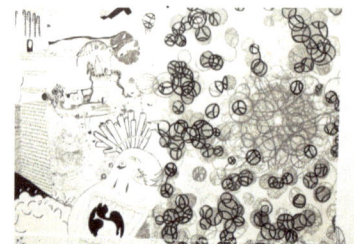
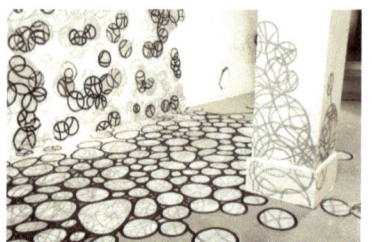
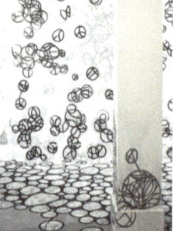

Ken Lovell

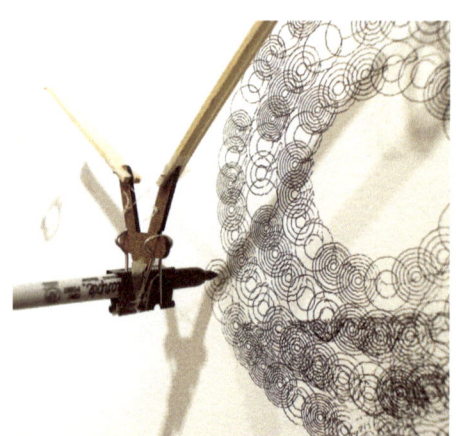

E ven though the Scrawl project was a simple one, artists found ways to complicate and stir things up. Ken Lovell was one of these, pushing the boundaries as to what media we would accept and creating an elaborate set of rationales and preparatory processes which guided his approach. His drawing robot was very popular with audiences from the first. It was like watching a small hummingbird intent on its work; seeing it form its perfect circles was quite hypnotic.

Lovell writes: "From the opening of the show I tried to develop the idea of drawing in reaction to a given framework. During the opening I set up a drawing machine that used code to create a ground…. The machine drawing served two purposes: first to generate a visual catalyst within the field and second to cover a significant area of the overall working space autonomously. One of the challenges I faced in producing the Scrawl drawing was that I had a limited amount of time to complete a complex idea. I used the autonomous drawbot as a proxy to be present, disturbing the space, while I had to be elsewhere.

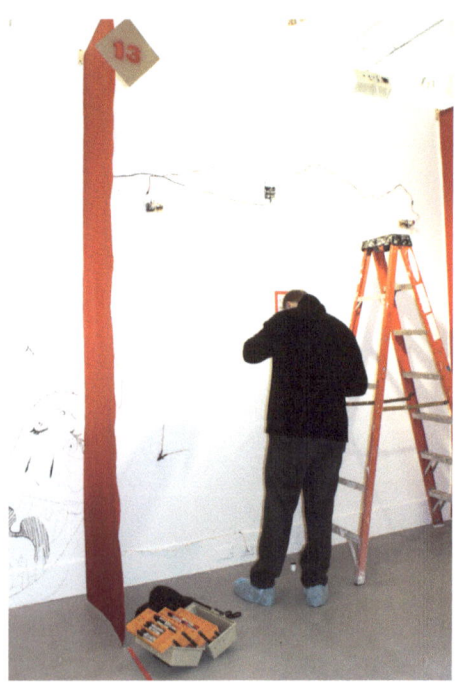

"I started with other artists encroaching around the outside perimeter of my working space and a programmed drawbot densely despoiling the interior of the working space. In order to link the two areas of activity I needed to create a field that could mediate between the irregular mechanical marks at the interior of the picture and whatever my neighbors were doing to the East and West. Initially it seemed like a duel for visual dominance at the periphery of each person's space, with the bloody banners marking the bleeding edges. Over time, as we got to know each other, through proximity, and acceptance of each other's peculiarities, both in terms of style and approach, the show became a great way to meet my co-artists and to learn about them through their work.

"… The origin of the exquisite corpse project, in Dadaistic practice, is intended to disrupt reason, to pervert our natural inclination to make sense out of visual experience and in so doing create a new 'sense' born from that fractured chaos … The tension that this practice creates at the border of each artist's practice was evident in the Scrawl show. The transitions from work to work were sometimes barely noticeable, flowing elegantly in a stylistic pas de deux, while other works butted against each other like a banana and a brick wall."

Ken Lovell received his BFA in Printmaking from Indiana University and his MFA in Painting from Yale University. Early in his career, he became fascinated with the possibilities that computers presented to art making. This combination of printmaking experience and computer savvy led to his being the first person hired for Yale's Digital Media Center for the Arts, where he is currently the Technical Director. ■

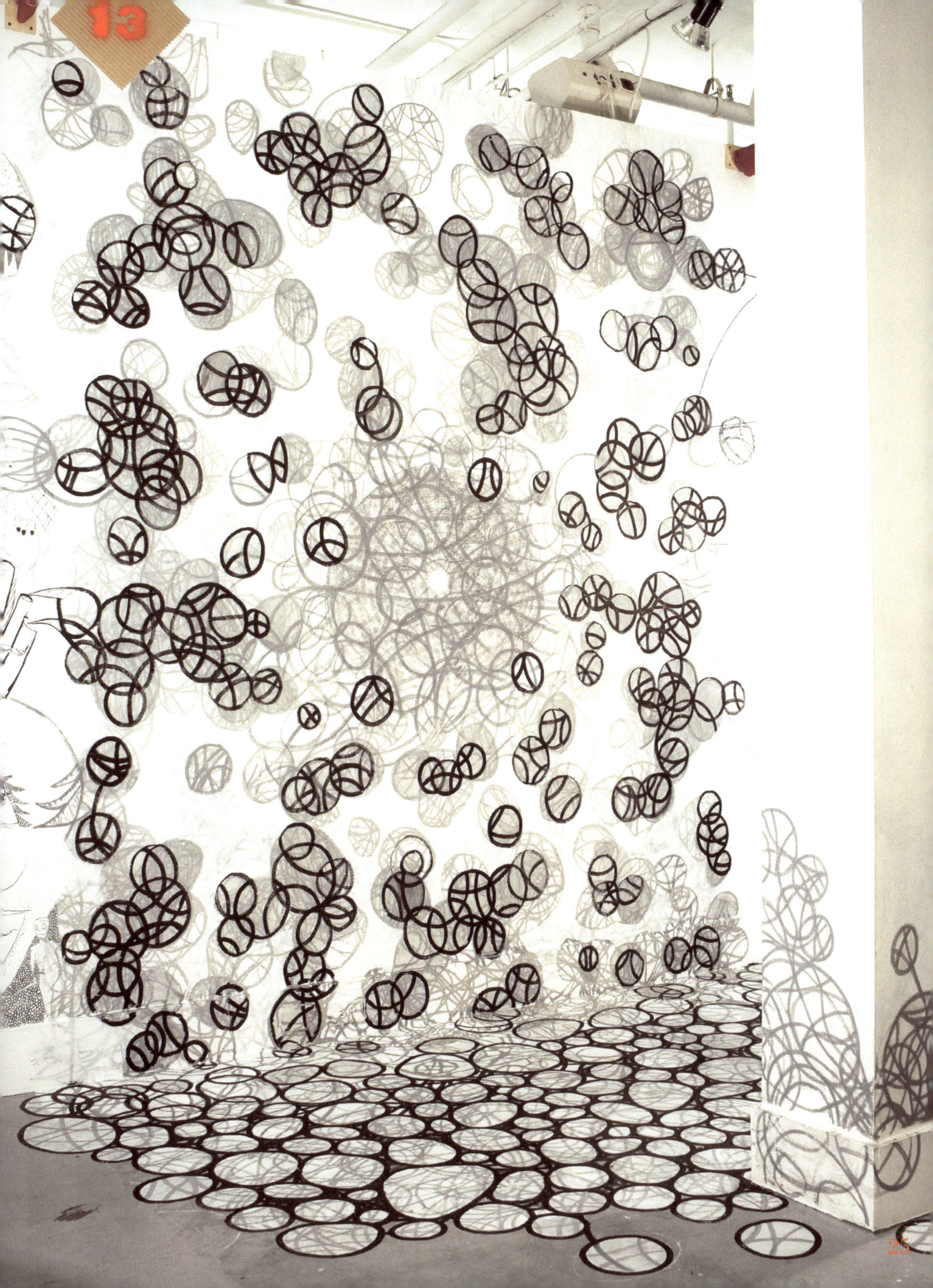

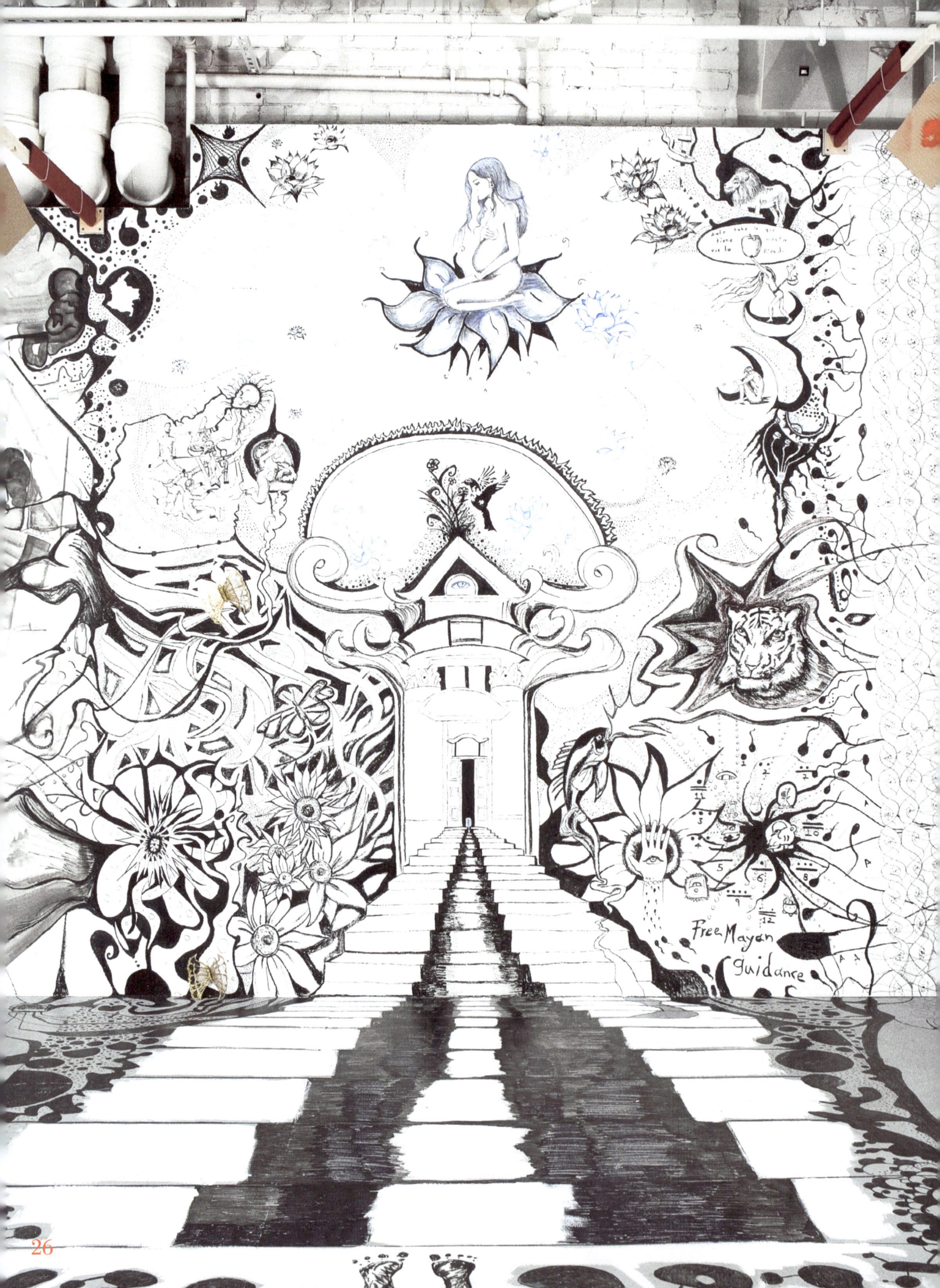

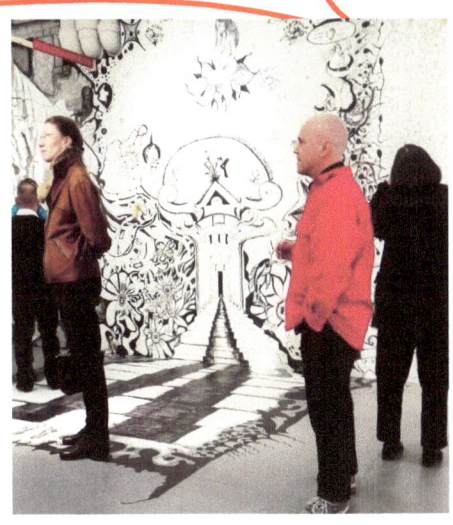

Andres Madariaga

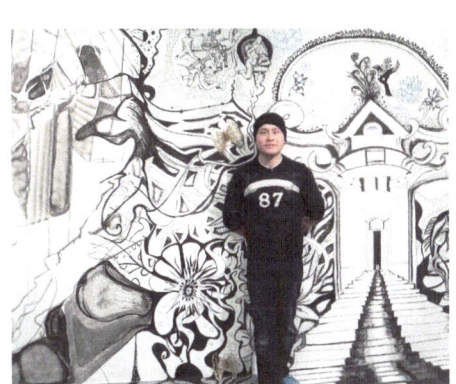

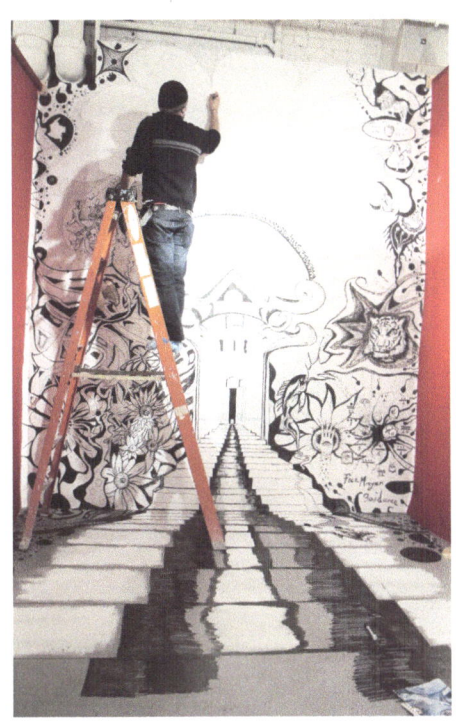

Andres Madariaga states that the appeal of drawing in its ability to transform an idea into a tangible emotion. He is inspired by writers like Gabriel Garcia Marquez, who mix the real and the surreal.

He writes of his work for Scrawl: "It all started with the idea of cyclical life where only emotions were visible. I had a person in mind from the beginning and this created many emotions and clues that can be found in the piece. In a way, it is a monument to love, but also to death, loss and struggle. Each petal symbolizes a different part of life: regret, love, death, desire, unrequited love, but I wanted to keep the spiritual part in the center. The woman symbolizes the union of all religions that are mainly focused on men. In this case, the pregnant woman is the center of all life and the bringer of all things: the muse and the inspiration. I wanted to create a path into a human soul sort of like stepping into a window and peeking inside someone else's ideas and emotions, so I combined the sub-conscious with reality into one imaginary realm.

"The piece invites you to enter on to the stairs and find your center, your guidance. It welcomes you to look at life without any attachments and to look into the essence, the spirit, and the soul of all people, not their appearance. This is a journey that I feel we all ought to take. So: I invite you to step in, and find your own symbols and embrace yourself into the dream.

"Growing up in two cultures has always been difficult for me, never fitting in to one or the other, and with art it has been no different. I used to think that background made no difference in making art; that an artist is no different if he comes from South America or somewhere else in the world. With time I have learned that there are some things that change and some that never do: differences appear, many of them are subliminal and come from deep in the subconscious. However, at the end, the actual work can surpass any barrier that society or our own stereotypes can make, because even though art is a lie, it holds no lies. It is our own crude judge and also our most intimate and pure savior."

Andres Madariaga was born in Colombia and lives and works in New Haven. He has studied at Gateway Community College, is an Educational Center for the Arts alumni, and has participated in the Cooper Union summer program. He has received the Elizabeth Greeley Memorial Fund portfolio award, and first prize in the COLT poetry recitation contest. Madariaga has exhibited his work in solo and group exhibitions around New Haven, CT. ■

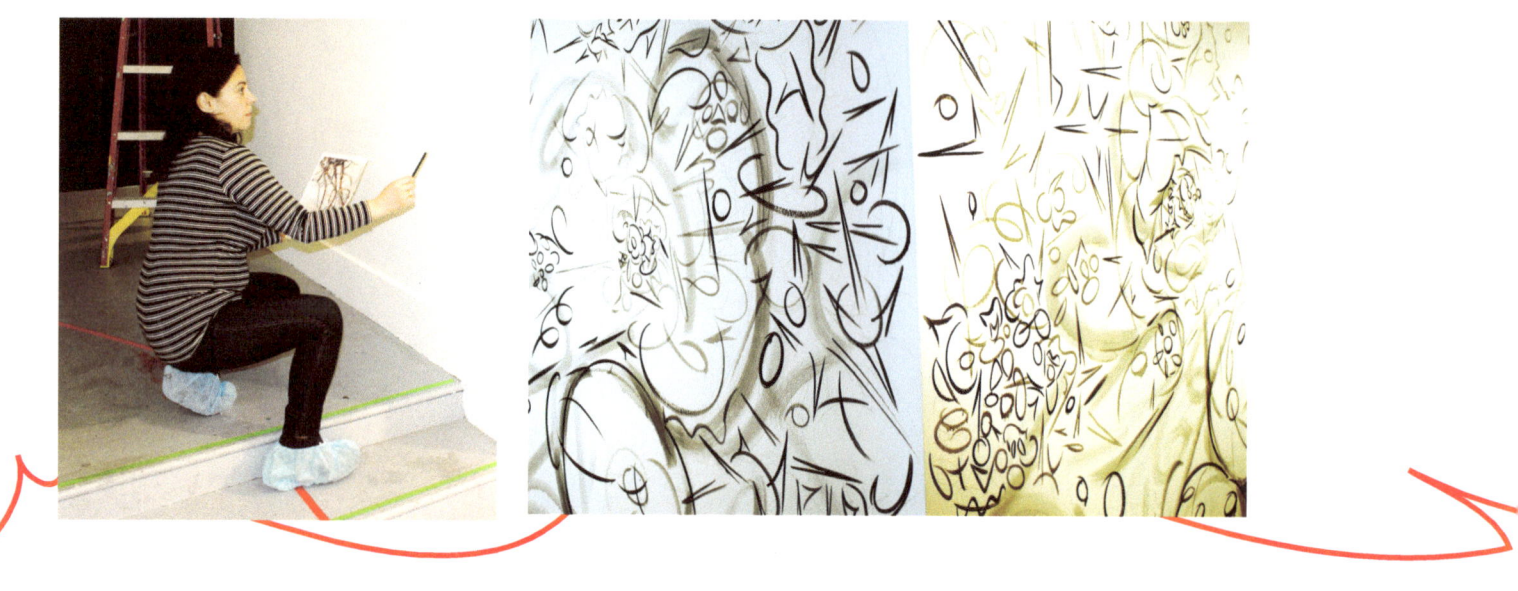

Melissa Marks

Melissa Marks is known for her vast wall drawings that jump with action and movement. She filled her section so quickly that it was necessary to extend her space around the corner, a move which allowed for a spatial play that made her work dance off of the walls she was drawing on and fire sparks across to Maegen McElderry's free-falling miniature people.

She writes of her Scrawl experience: "I have compared the drawn mark and its 'heroic' history to a superhero. What I love about Scrawl is the opportunity to perform drawing in a collaborative context, like being a member of the Drawing Justice League. All the usual artist superpowers are honored, everyone engaged in their distinct practice, interior thoughts and motivations made visible, bringing idiosyncratic attributes to the cause, with the outcome resting completely on the interdependence of diverse skills. As much as I believe drawing is 'performed,' I also believe that once a mark is made visible, it reveals something essentially human—a worthwhile cause for the Drawing Justice League.

"I found the game aspects of Scrawl to be exceedingly fun. Being interrupted by other art is one of the luxuries of being an artist …. How fantastic to have live artists interrupt you mid-practice. How fantastic to incorporate interruption into your work by agreeing that the borders of your piece are completely up for grabs. Wall drawing is a regular part of my practice. The drawing is reactive to the shape of the architecture, the given context. In the past there has been some time for rumination. The slow incorporation of the particular narrative qualities of the space into my imagination … With Scrawl that process was accelerated. I didn't really have time to let the shape

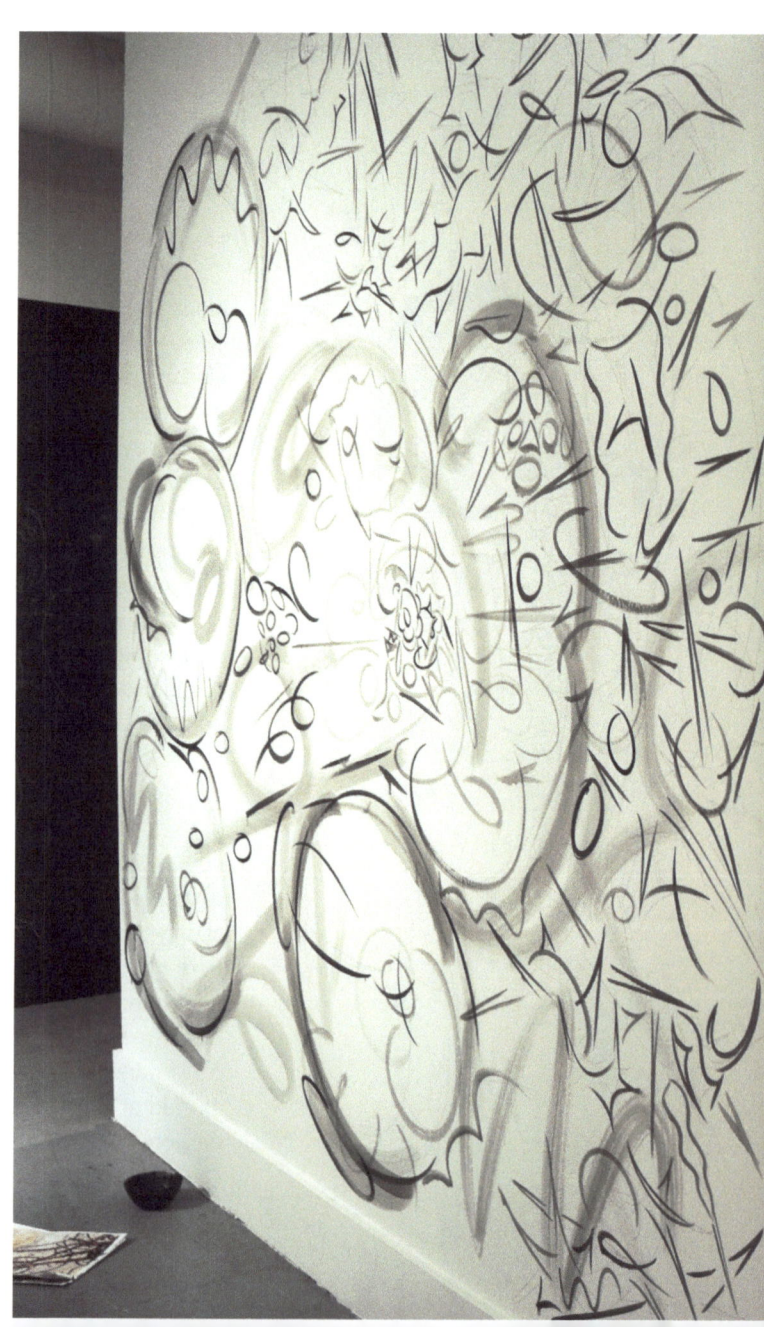

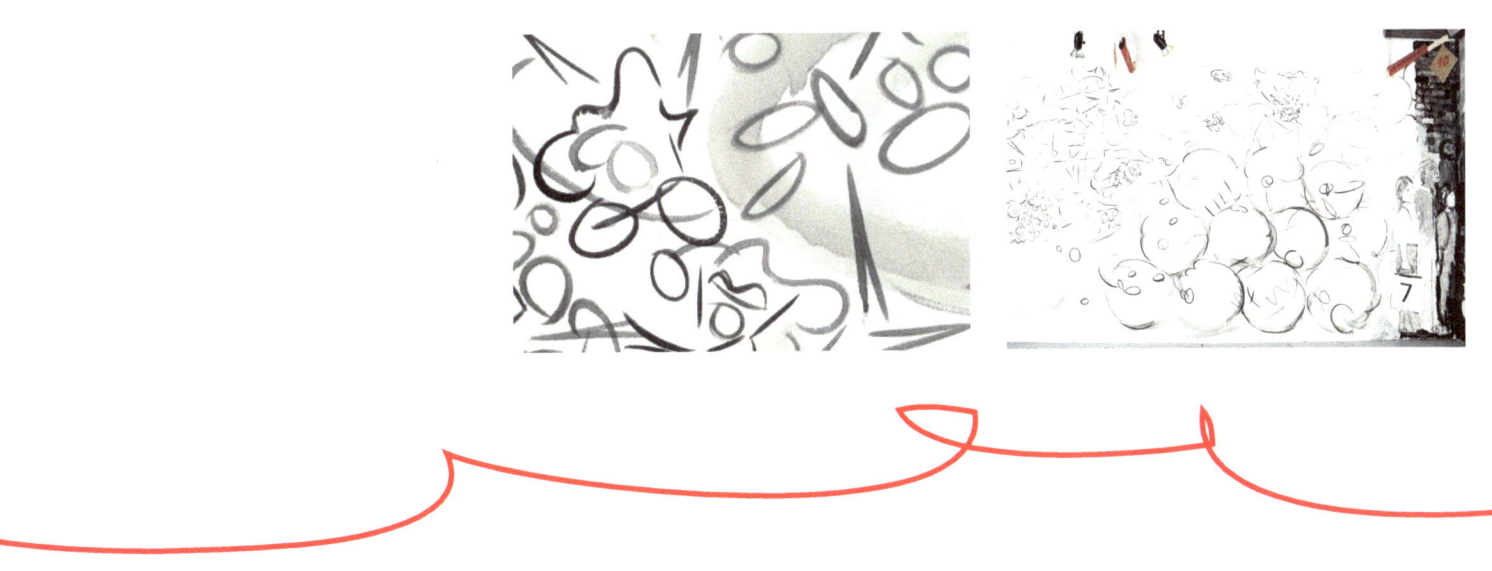

of my space seep into my consciousness. All the decisions were immediate, all go. I enjoyed that new challenge. It absolutely shifted my approach to my next large-scale wall project, a site that had been floating around in my mind for almost a year. Once drawing happens on the scale of a wall it becomes social. It occurs in the realm of physical interaction. Conversation, language, human dramas are natural components of the experience. Scrawl seemed to be continually acknowledging that throughout its evolution. Very cool."

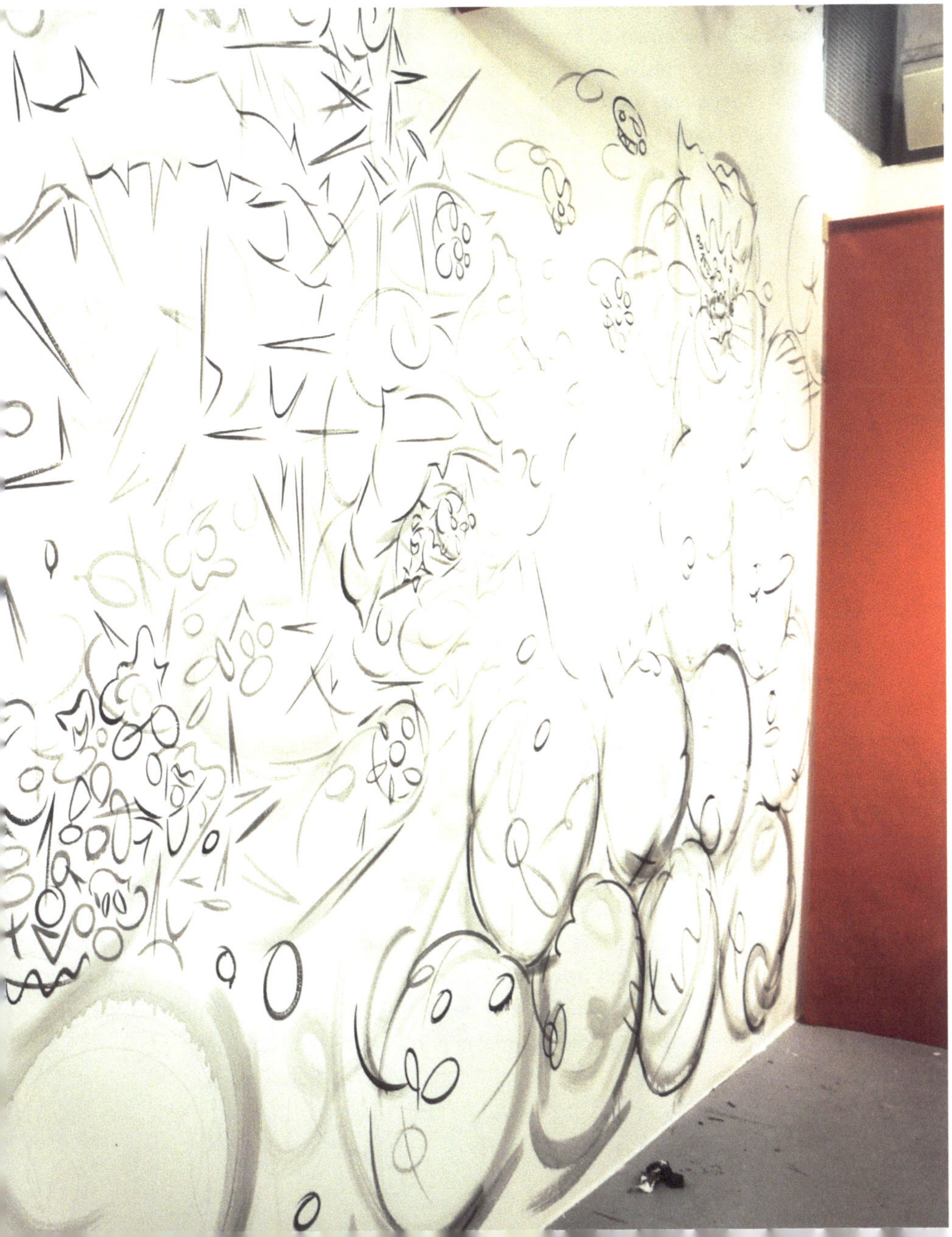

Melissa Marks received her MFA from the Yale School of Art and has exhibited throughout the United States, London, Germany, and Spain, including Vassar College, Poughkeepsie, NY; Site Gallery, Sheffield, UK; Nicole Klagsbrun Gallery, New York; P.S.1 Contemporary Art Center, New York; and The Aldrich Contemporary Art Museum, Ridgefield, CT. In 2007 she was commissioned for a solo exhibition of a site-specific work at the Bloomberg SPACE in London. Articles on her work have appeared in such publications as *Bomb*, *The New York Times*, *Almanach zur Jungen Kunst*, and Taiwan's *Freedom Magazine*. Marks, upon finishing her work for Scrawl immediately headed to Andalucía, Spain, where she made a permanent wall installation for the Cortijada los Gázquez. ■

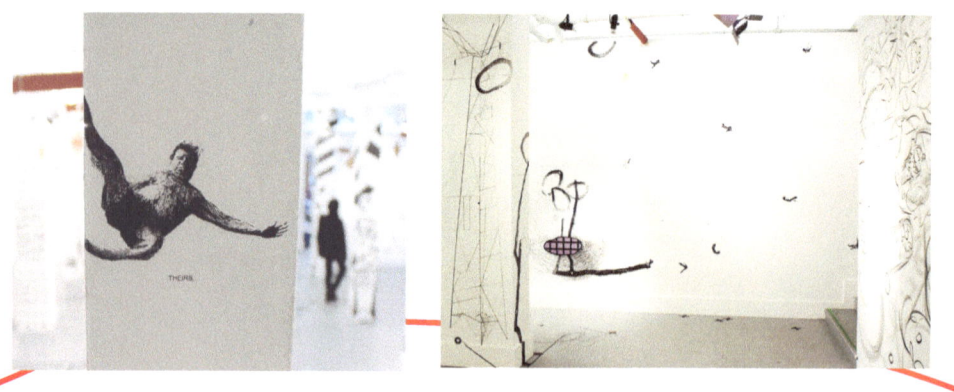

Maegen McElderry eschewed the obvious and drew small, detailed figures free-falling across his wall and around the corner. He joined his work with that of neighbor Anna Broell Bresnick and tackled the floor with restraint and aplomb. His piece for Scrawl balanced white space and drawn mark in a way that was unique and musical in its precision.

Here are his thoughts about Scrawl: "I expected crazy, and found crazier. The nature of this group ranged from serious to delirious, which bracketed everything that I did, allowing me to feel comfortable with this social space.

"I assumed my work would be large and gestural, instead, it turned out to be small, delicate, and momentary. This work pushed me beyond where I assumed I was at this point in my life. I have always only worked in my studio. I have never had so many people look at my work. I feel like I quickly conquered my self-consciousness and settled into a state of productivity. It was creativity on demand, and for me, that is tough.

"… I was hoping to draw people within nose-distance to the wall, there you could see the fetish of the pen tip. I remained black and white so that I could really dig into the concept and not distract anyone with a random bit of color or material. I feel my work turned out like text on a page: type font is important, but the individual reading mostly wins."

Maegen McElderry

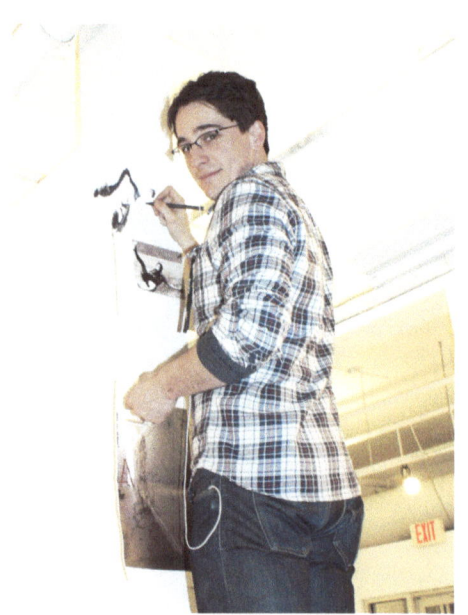

In terms of negotiating the intersections he writes: "It was a blindfolded tango. Since I only had one neighbor (Bresnick), it felt as if we were in freefall and each time someone reached for a hand, it was there. We were organelles, and somehow, out of the nature of things, we came to function, beautifully."

And about the work as whole: "I will be honest, I expected more drawing on the floor. However, everything that was rendered, was given love, and therefore needs no validation. Simply amazing. This is a show that I will cherish. In a way, its removal is relaxing. Now the memories must muscle their way through our heads."

Maegen McElderry is a practicing architect who received his M. Arch from the University of Minnesota. Maegen helped to devise and construct Scrawl's structural apparatus and was an indispensible member of the design team. His imagination, effort and skill were indelibly imprinted on the exhibit; all of the visual aspects of the show owe a huge debt to him and his ingenuity. He has exhibited work in Connecticut and Minnesota and is the 2010 recipient of the Ralph Rapson Travelling Fellowship. His artistic process and aesthetic intent is to celebrate the mark, by any means necessary. He takes a playful approach to surfaces and explores the subtle undertones of imprint, trace, and subtraction. ■

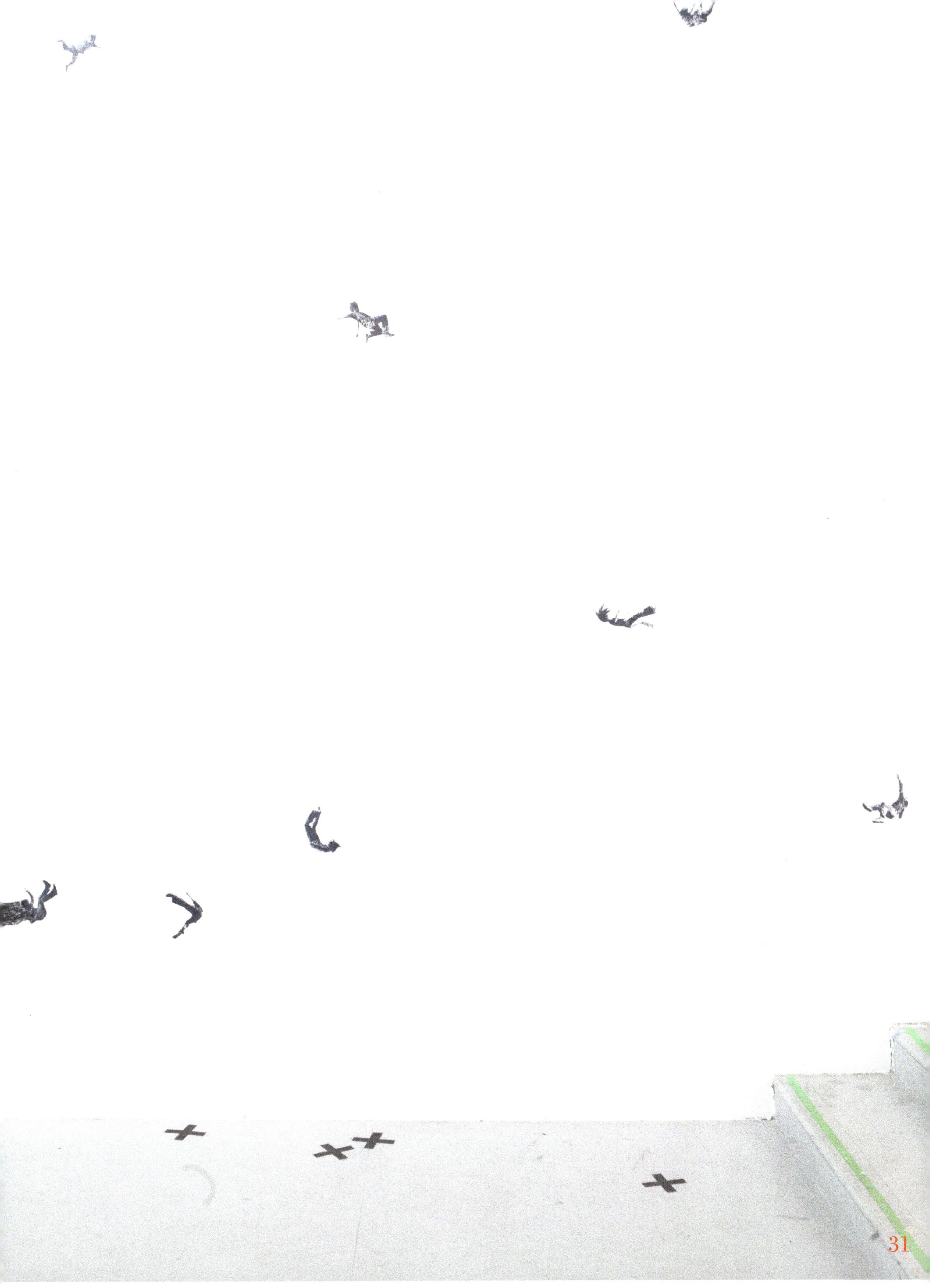

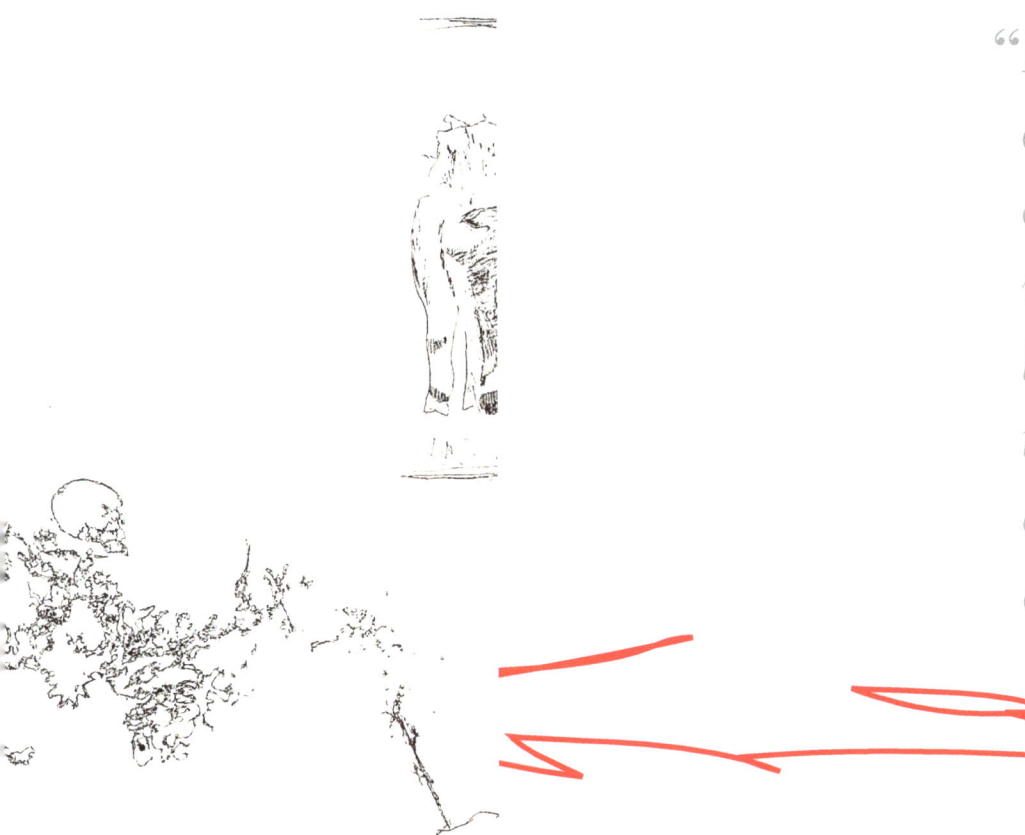

*"I work with
a great deal
of line so I
was naturally
looking for
intersections I
could stretch
and expand…"*

Tim Nikiforuk

Tim Nikiforuk's work uses and investigates various biological systems and structures, to produce drawings that rise and envelope the space. His particular working process was a bit difficult for collective interactions, in the sense that he needed to work in the dark with a projector. Thus, he often ended up working in his space alone. However, Tim was really adept at meshing with the wildly different works alongside him, and seemed to relish the collective parts of the game, curling neatly into the hair of James Rose's young woman, and smoking and bubbling out of the pamphlet of Laura Gardner's reading man.

As Nikiforuk describes it: "I found functioning as a collective entity rather easy…. I really felt my piece was merely a connection point for the two beside me…. The scale was larger and I was obviously working directly on the wall, but other than that it was very similar to my studio practice…. For me it was simply a process of extension. I work with a great deal of line so I was naturally looking for intersections I could stretch and expand…

"I personally felt no inclination to fill my entire space. I could see the one-upmanship happening amongst a number of the artists, so I consciously kept things as direct as I could. No question that people became competitive with respect to drawing the audience's attention away from the whole and on to their individual pieces. I just used it as an opportunity to go the other way and embraced less equals more."

And in terms of Scrawl as a whole: "I was skeptical about the outcome of the work as it was being produced, but in the end I felt it came together fairly well. Interesting concept paired with a number of really engaging components…."

Tim Nikiforuk received a BFA from the University of Calgary, Canada, and an MFA from the University of Connecticut, Storrs. He has exhibited in solo and group exhibitions in Connecticut, New York, and Canada. Nikiforuk currently teaches art at Quinebaug Valley Community College and the University of New Haven. ■

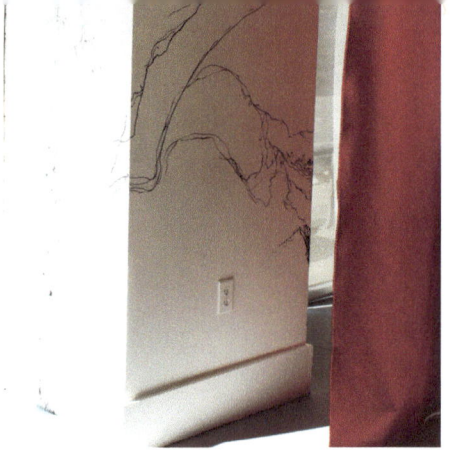

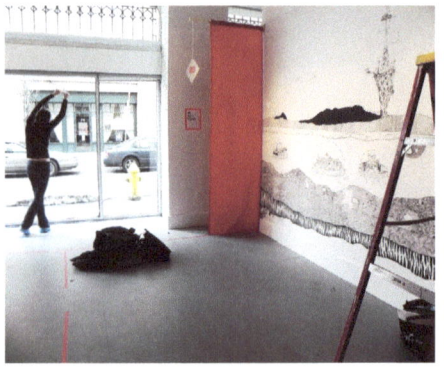

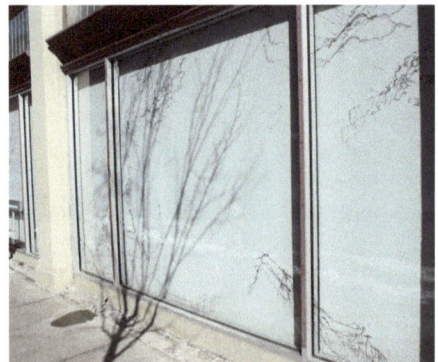

K erry O'Grady's work draws from "the experience of time as unhinged, indeterminate, and discontinuous and from the interstitial moments of perception between those that can be concretely described. A mark immediately becomes a trace of the past, embodying the spontaneous movement that made it." This is very much a process-oriented, time-based approach, close to dance, and was immediately evident in how she confronted her space for Scrawl:

"Since I was working on the window, I thought about the act of 'performing a drawing' a lot. Being aware of the potential of a viewer seeing the process—or the performance—of the drawing, instead of just the product of drawing, gave me a lot to question … The marker kept everything in the immediate present. It made the act of drawing more of a performance of the present. It also altered the reinvestigation of previously-made marks.…"

O'Grady worked on a large window space, connecting inside to out as much as with her neighbors. Her space, unlike the others, was very much interactive with the light, the

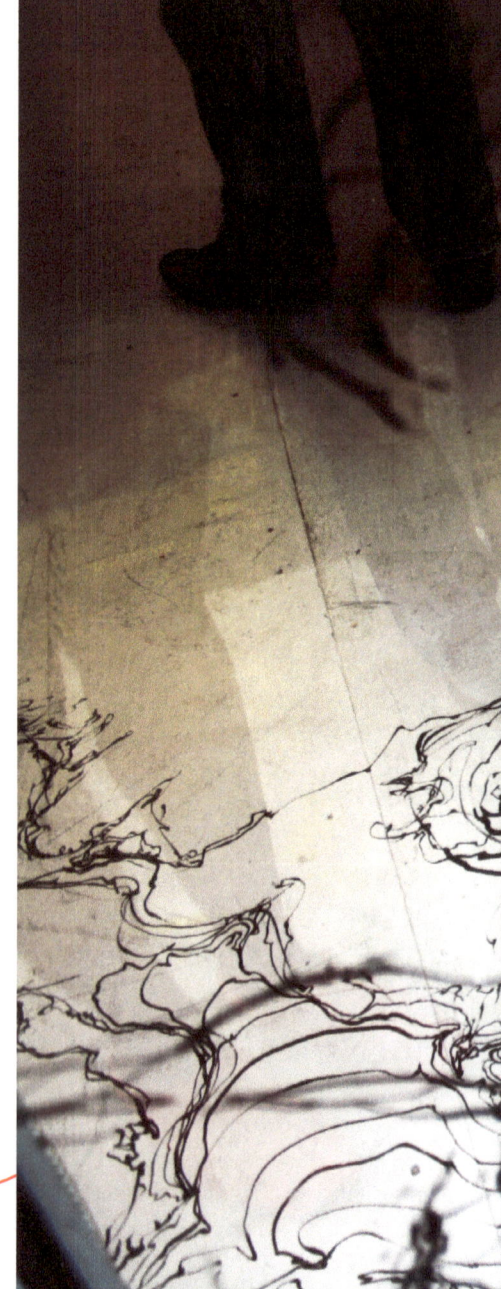

Kerry O'Grady

time of day, the weather. In this sense her collaboration took place outside of the gallery space, but there were still, flanking her on either side, two teams drawing on walls. She stuck rigorously to the rules of the game and seemed to enjoy the minimalism imposed by these rules:

"I liked experimenting within these limits. Because the marker only created lines of one value, and those lines all rested on the surface in a non-layered way, the material restrictions pushed me towards a process based on creating a record of movement, which reinforced the role of the window. Both of these elements served a performative approach to drawing over an imagistic one. The process was great. To me, this whole project was about the investigation that arose through the process."

"I think the balance of artistic autonomy and collaboration was interesting in this project. Different people arrived at different ways of relating to their neighbors.... I extended lines towards the other's walls to see if they'd get picked up—and my neighbors incorporated some of them into their work. One group did the same for me, and I used some of their lines. It was like we had extended each other a branch."

O'Grady has an MFA from UMass Amherst. She has also studied at the Museum School in Boston and the University of Dar es Salaam, Tanzania, and holds a BA Cum Laude in Art and Anthropology from Connecticut College. She has exhibited throughout the northeast and in Canada. She is currently Director of the Seton Art Gallery, and Lecturer, University of New Haven, where she lives and works. ■

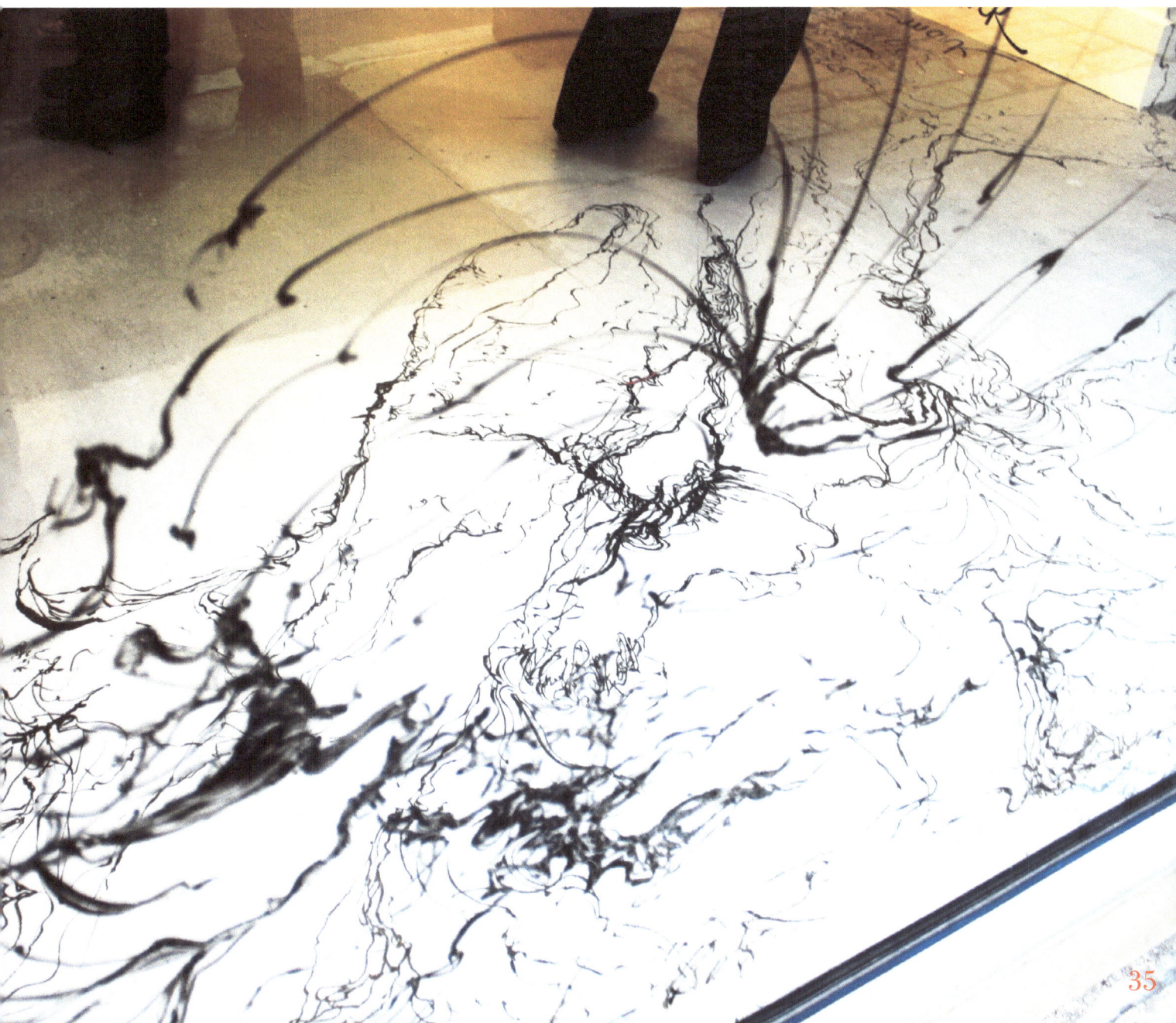

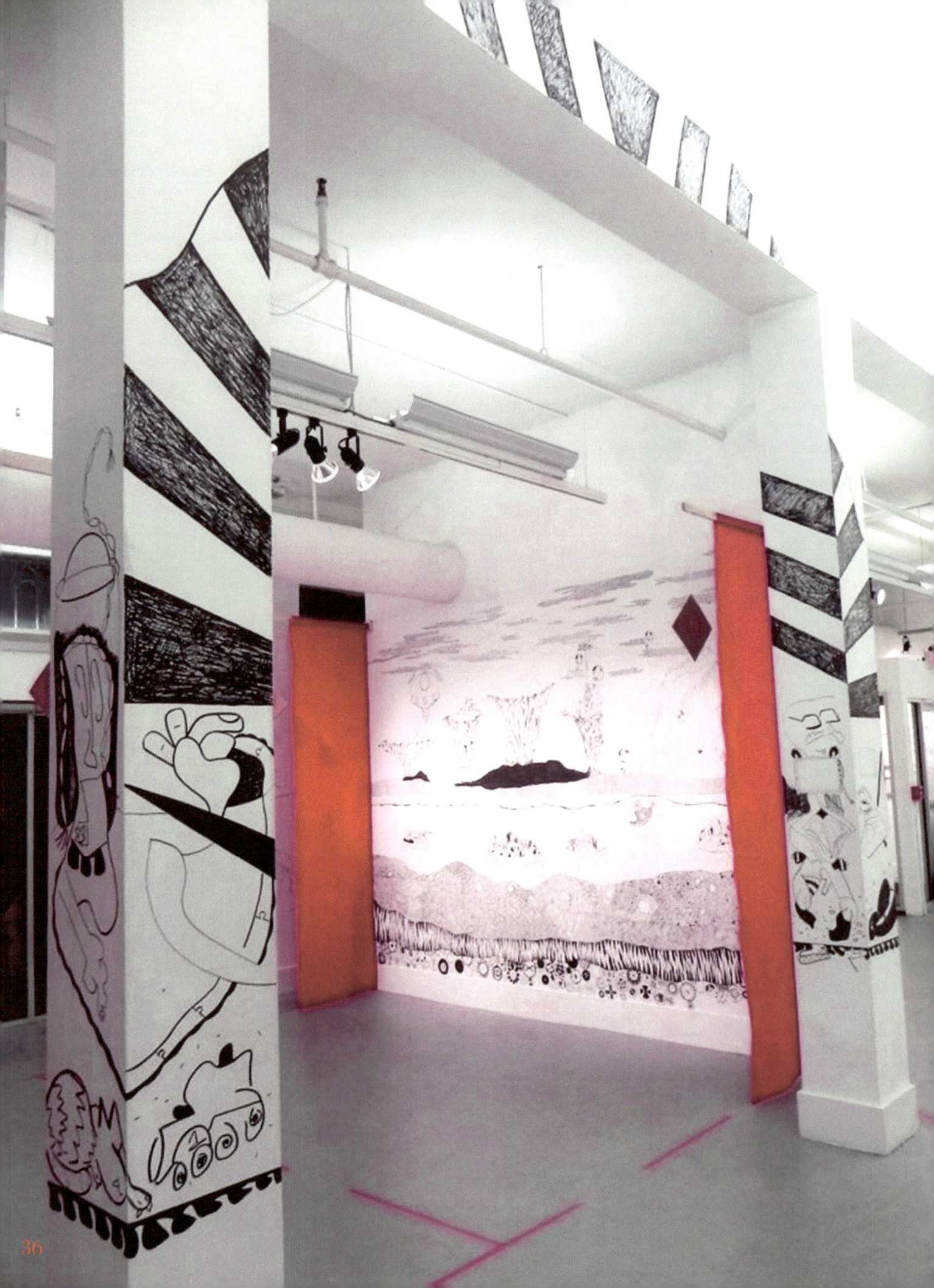

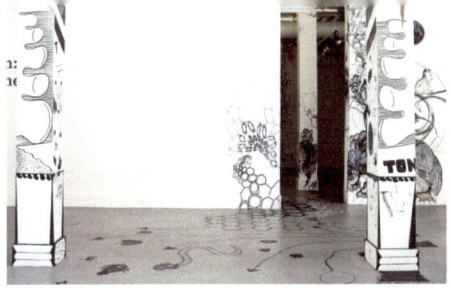
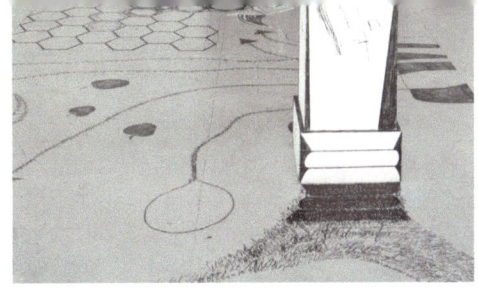

Daniel Rios Rodriguez

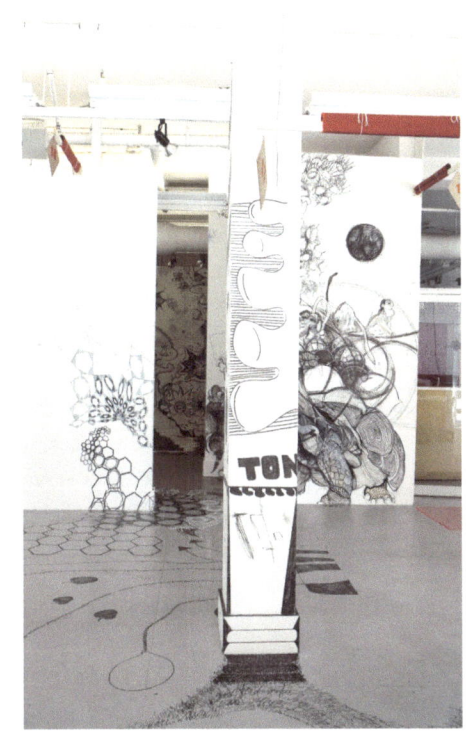

In addition to having his own section, Daniel Rios Rodriquez worked with the Coop high school students and artist Rebecca Salter on their project. This led to a double vision of Scrawl for him, as a self-determined project, and working as a team. For his own portion of Scrawl, Rodriquez daringly chose a section of two columns and a ceiling soffit, which he visually transformed into an arch. This became the entryway into the realms of Team Tele, the Futurists, and Kerry O'Grady's window work.

Rodriguez took this not-very-promising stretch of real estate and ran with it, making a work at once spontaneous, bold and rhythmic: a vibrant entryway. His work was unique in its engagement of the ceiling (off limits for drawing for this project, for practical reasons) and really used the height of the space to great effect. Although he says he did not enjoy working on the grey floors as much, he had his images flowing back and forth to the territory of the Futurists, who then had their line of streaming survivalist ants trickling into Kerry's adjacent space as well.

Keeping anything a secret from Rodriguez was very difficult, as he was always on a very high ladder: no amount of partitions and screens available to us could really prevent him from knowing his neighbor's output. However, he used this to great advantage, playing with it and creating a cohesive mélange of the disparate activities surrounding him. He playfully riffed on what he knew of what the others were up to, absorbing and echoing back a version filtered through his eye and hand.

He writes of his experience: "Most of my work is small to medium-sized paintings. It was nice to stretch out some of my usual ideas onto the wall, or in my case, tall columns … I didn't mind working amongst other artists and thought there was always a good energy about the space. A sense of competition in my view is always present whether one admits it or not. I think all artists want to put out their best work so sizing up the work of others as it progresses feeds the creative spirit…. I was impressed overall with the entire project. Even in the sections where drawings didn't necessarily communicate, the overall visual impact was pretty refreshing as a whole."

Daniel Rios Rodriguez received a BFA from the University of Illinois in Chicago in 2005 and an MFA from the Yale School of Art in 2007. Rodriguez recently had a solo exhibition at White Columns in New York. He worked as installation assistant for Sol LeWitt's Wall Drawing 11 at the Yale University Art Gallery, where he was also a gallery teacher and education assistant. Formerly project director at the San Antonio Arts in Education Initiative, Rodriguez is now teaching at the Coop Arts High School's after-school program in New Haven, CT. ■

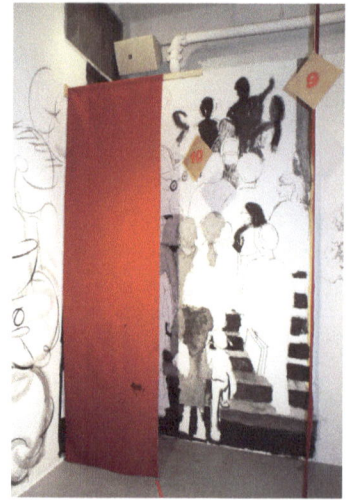

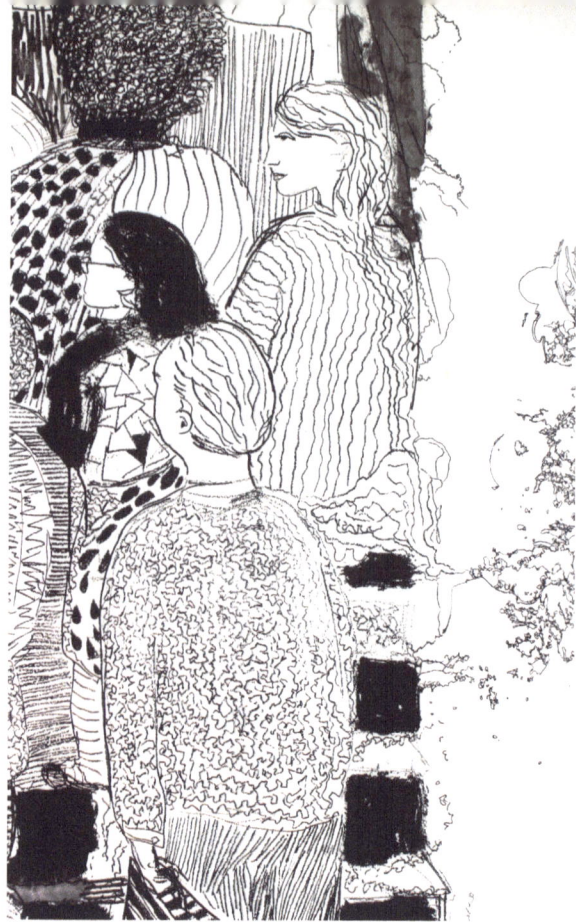

James Rose

For Scrawl James Rose produced a vibrant, painterly scene of people ascending the stairs from the subway (which is the source for much of his output; many of his drawings take place on trains, metros, and other public transport systems). His space was a tall corner and he was adjacent to Mellissa Marks's flowing burst of visual vitamin C and Tim Nikiforuk's sparkling dancing line. Thus, his own works focus on vertical movement, provided a jolt from the strong current of horizontal eddying flowing around him. His work, textured and nuanced, offered a dense urban flavor to his section of the space.

"I have worked on large scale works on walls before, but never in a group and never with markers or ink. It was a challenge, and when I saw other artists using different materials I jumped on it too. The large space with the thin line of a marker (Tim Nikiforuk's wall) made me have to think much differently, which was a good thing. As I said, it was difficult: I think in tones and light and dark. I do line drawings, but they still get smudgy and I will mix in a few fields of light, which is difficult to portray with line.

"After I realized I had gone outside the parameters set up for the project, I brought my process back into what had been expected by using pattern instead of light. I believe [complexity] is part of my aesthetic—I am definitely not a minimalist. I enjoy pattern, complex light and complex composition.

"I generally worked by myself; both of my adjacent artists were done early in the process. I did notice other artists working together and it was nice to see. I did incorporate the other artists on each side of me though, without their knowledge. I mimicked their style on the edges of my drawing, blending the different motifs. Most of the art was very impressive. It was a great project and good to see so many styles and techniques all together like that.

"There was some competition, but I think each approach was so different that it wasn't very high pressure. The one or two other figurative artists were encouraging if anything for me to continue and not make me feel like I was being too representational or non conceptual. Even though there was a concept behind my drawing ... I enjoyed everything very much. I was very fulfilled by this. It was a great learning experience and I feel I was part of something very cool."

James Rose paints and draws individuals and crowds in urban settings. He plays with the idea of the figure in relation to environment and focuses on multiculturalism, feminism and identity occurring in the interactive space of a city. Born in 1972, in Kinderhook, NY, Rose received his BFA from the Maine College of Art and has exhibited his work in Maine, New York, and California. ■

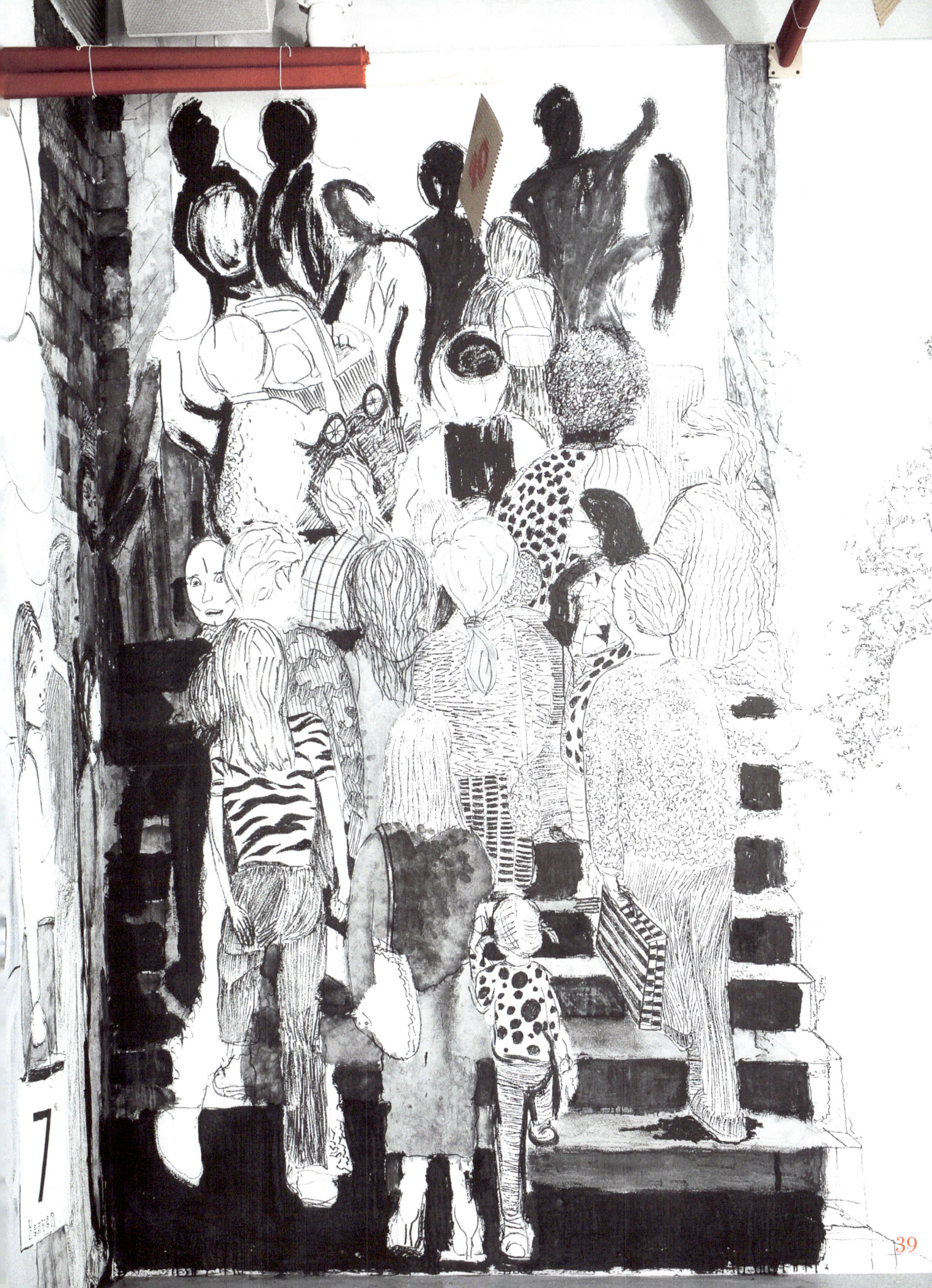

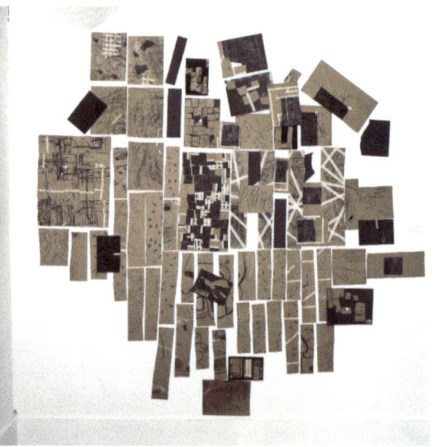

Rebecca Salter is an internationally renowned British artist whose conceptual drawing and printmaking have been exhibited worldwide. Salter's retrospective exhibition, Into the Light of Things, which ran concurrently with Scrawl at the Yale Center for British Art, investigated the centrality of drawing to art making.

Salter and students from Coop worked together to produce an animated film of the wall drawings they created during Scrawl as a part of her retrospective.

Salter was aided by Coop teachers/artists Daniel Rios Rodriguez and Kyle Sklar and YCBA educational curator Cyra Levinson to create a work that coexisted as portion of Scrawl and as the remnant of an animated drawing project with the students. Salter magnanimously agreed to work with us during her visits to New Haven and the collaboration received the generous support of the YBAC's education department for this portion of Scrawl.

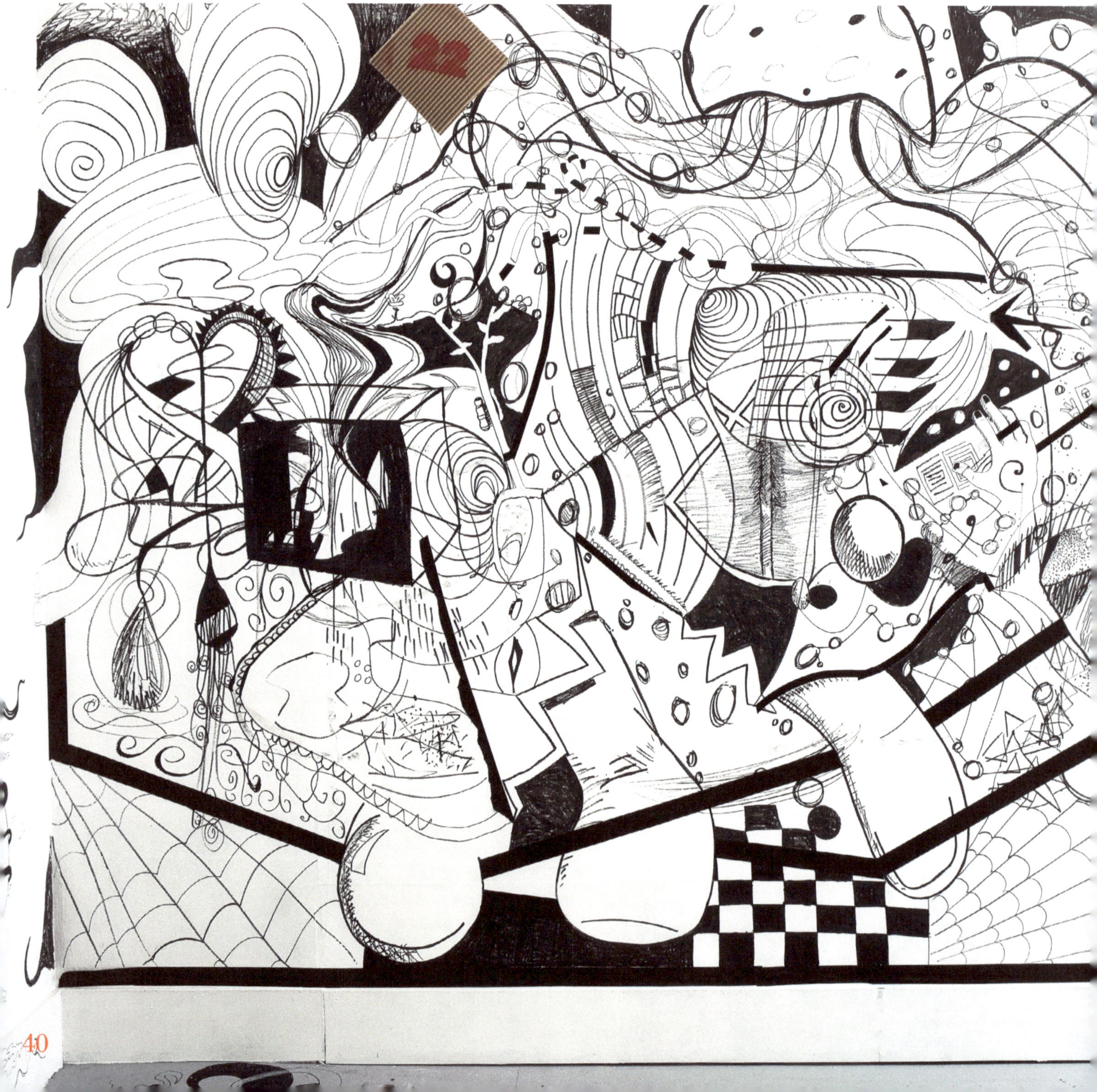

Over several sessions the students came, did drawing exercises relating to Rebecca's

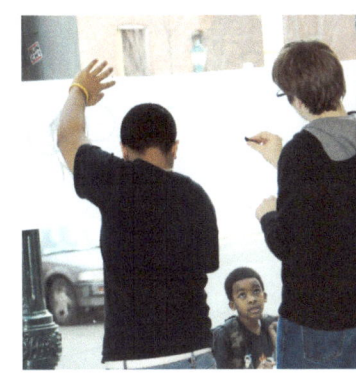

interests in ephemeral drawing,- working on subjects like shifting light, movement and gestural landscape. The work became the final panel in Scrawl's exquisite corpse.

Her exhibit into Into the light of things: Rebecca Salter works, 1981 – 2010 ran 3 February – 1 May, 2011 at the Yale Center for British Art and was accompanied by a monograph published by Yale University Press. Rebecca graduated from Bristol Polytechnic, Faculty of Art and Design and was a Research student at Kyoto City University of Arts, Japan, on a Leverhulme Scholarship. She has shown worldwide, most recently at Howard Scott Gallery, New York and Beardsmore Gallery in London. This year she was selected to participate in Tate Britain's Watercolour exhibition. Rebecca Salter has been the recipient of a Pollack Krasner award, and won first prize at the Cheltenham Open Drawing award. He work is in numerous collections including: the San Francisco Museum of Modern Art, The Portland Museum of Modern Art, The Tate Gallery, The Library of Congress, Washington DC, and The British Museum. ■

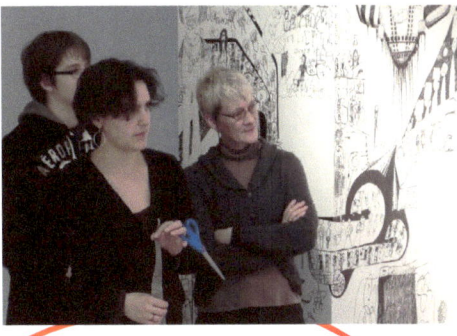

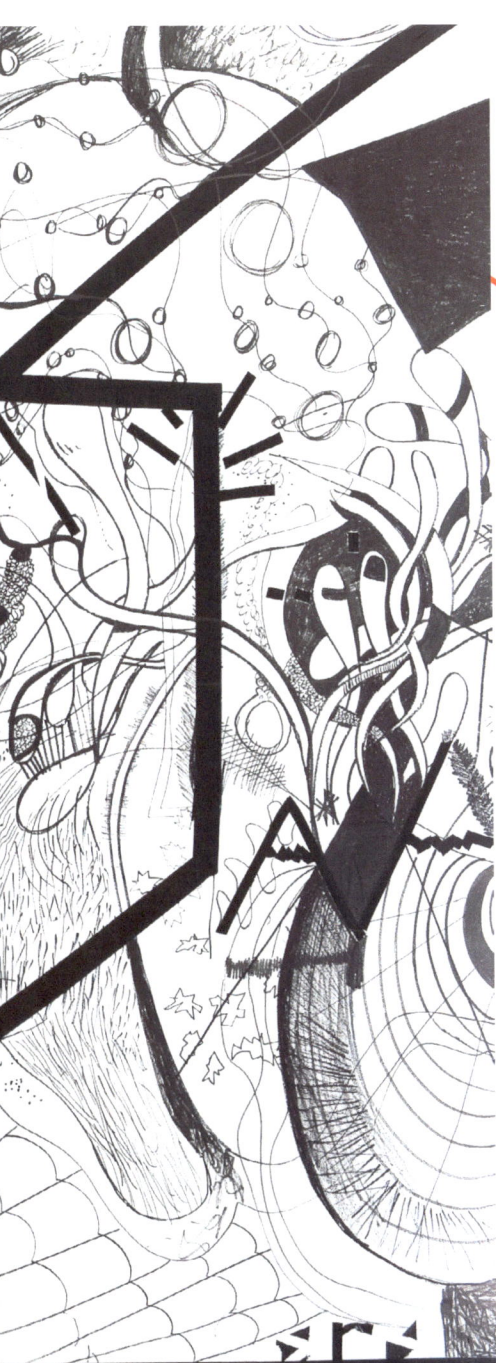

Rebecca Salter
with students from the Cooperative Arts & Humanities High School (Leon Acosta, Mackenzie Weborg, Cynthia Garcia, Melvin Morales, Kacie Piscatelli, and Max Wibert)

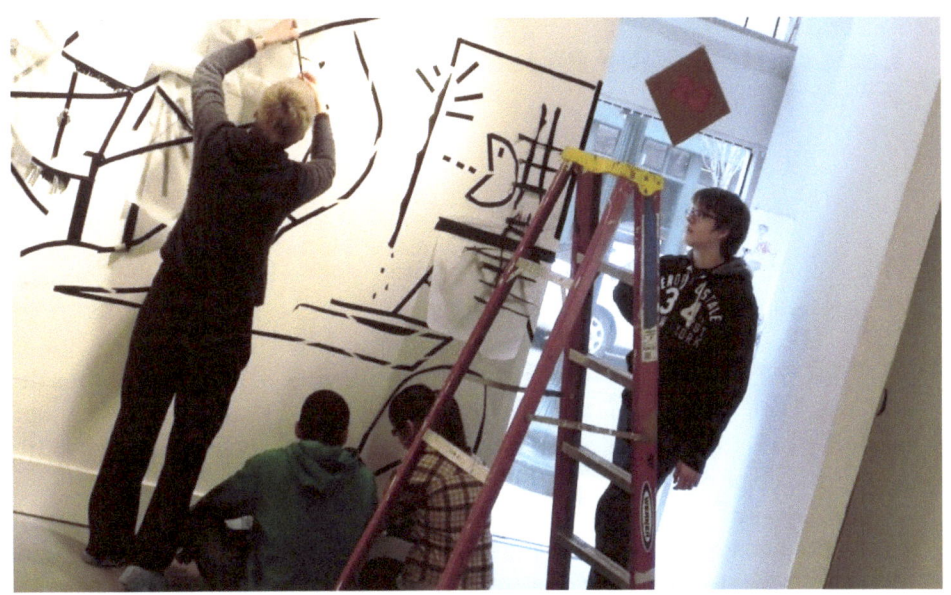

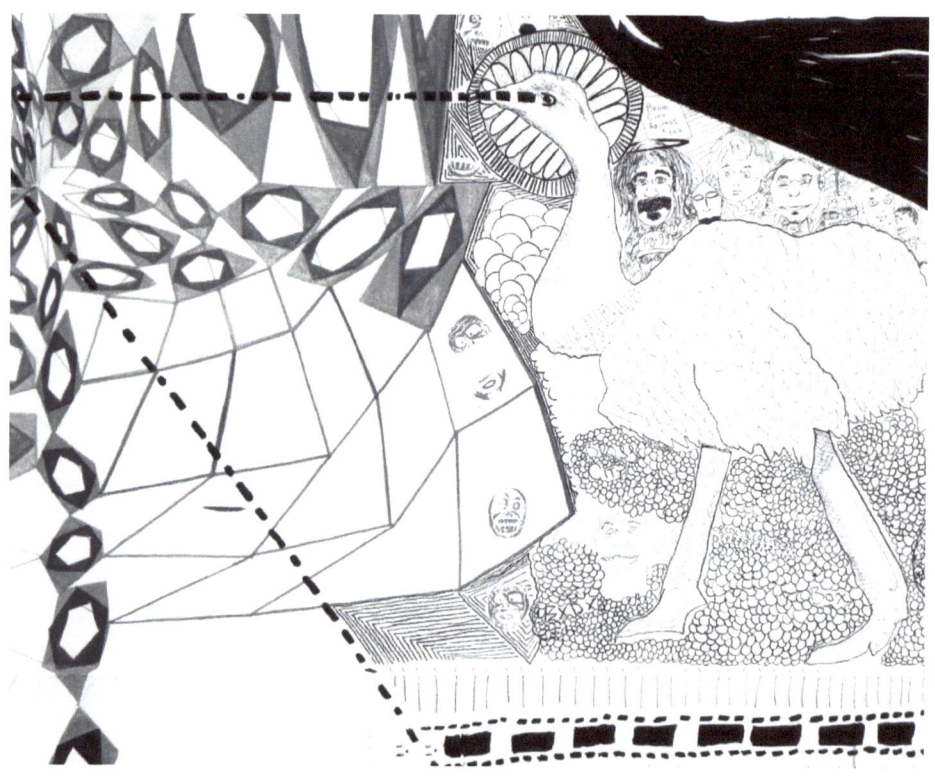

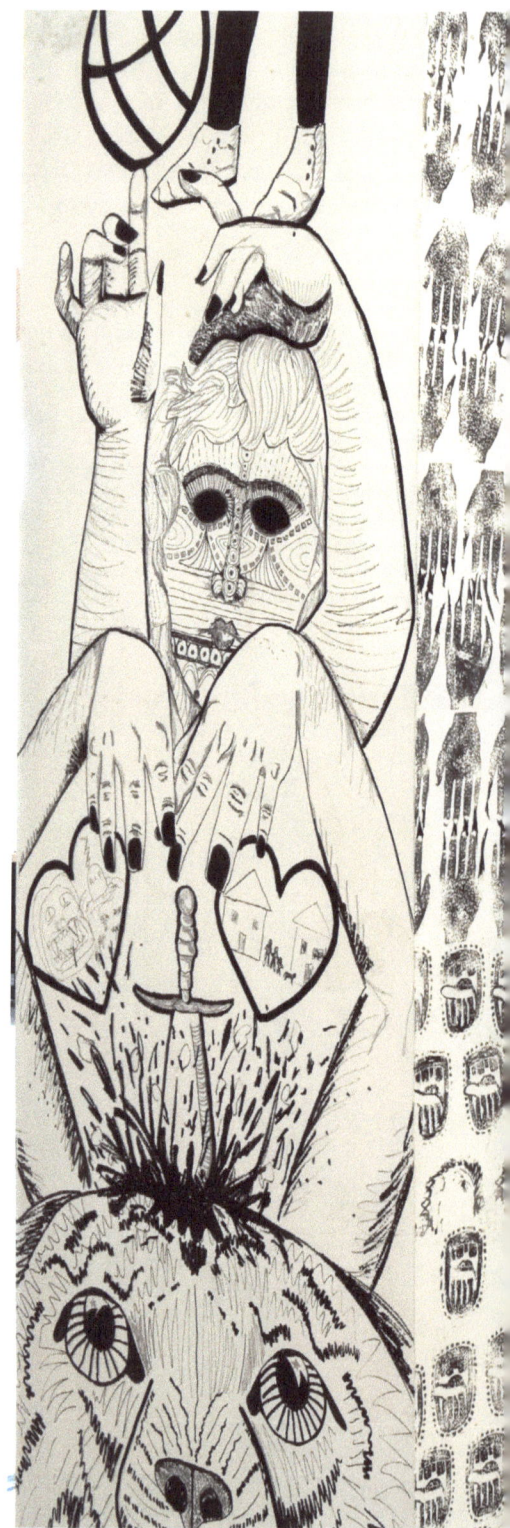

The Sausage Crew:

Larissa Hall, Mike Pitassi, and Michael Riley

The Sausage Crew has collaborated on multiple projects as their respective rap/hip-hop alter-egos: Queen Larita, M.C. Sausage and Dr. BOX. Through the combination of silent visual expression and rap theatricality, the Crew furthers its group identity with a focus on mastery and mayhem, challenging popular music and the stereotype of "the white rapper." They have been acquainted for ten-plus years and started honing their gifts for performance in 2008.

The Crew was a strong presence in the gallery, and created a highly-detailed symbolic work, full of surprising combinations and seemingly charged events from the history of their hometown, Waterbury, CT. Their drawing for Scrawl summoned up a James Ensor-esque sense of grotesque carnival: sprawling, eclectic and funny, their blighted animals, figures, and animated food had an undercurrent of festive menace.

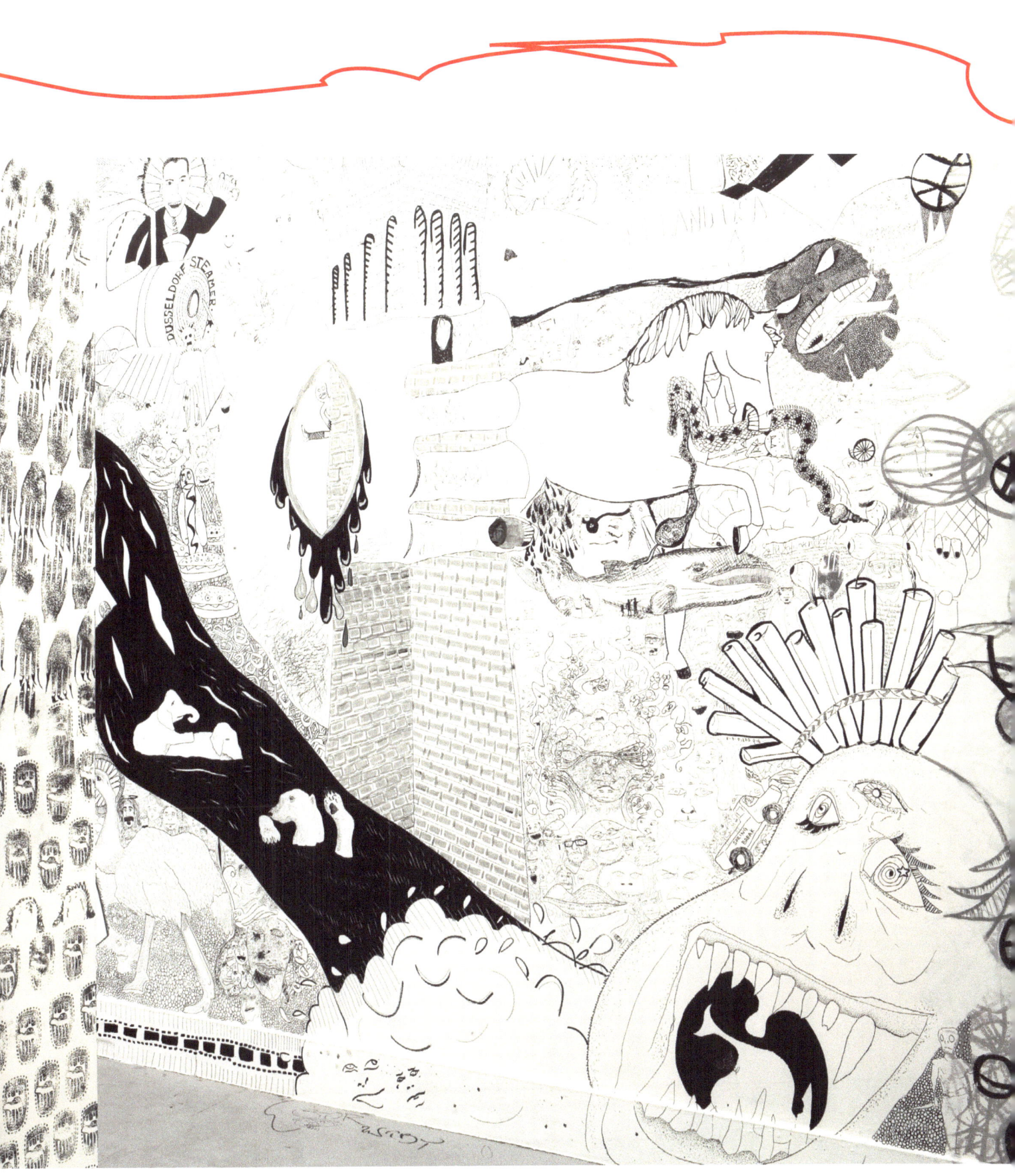

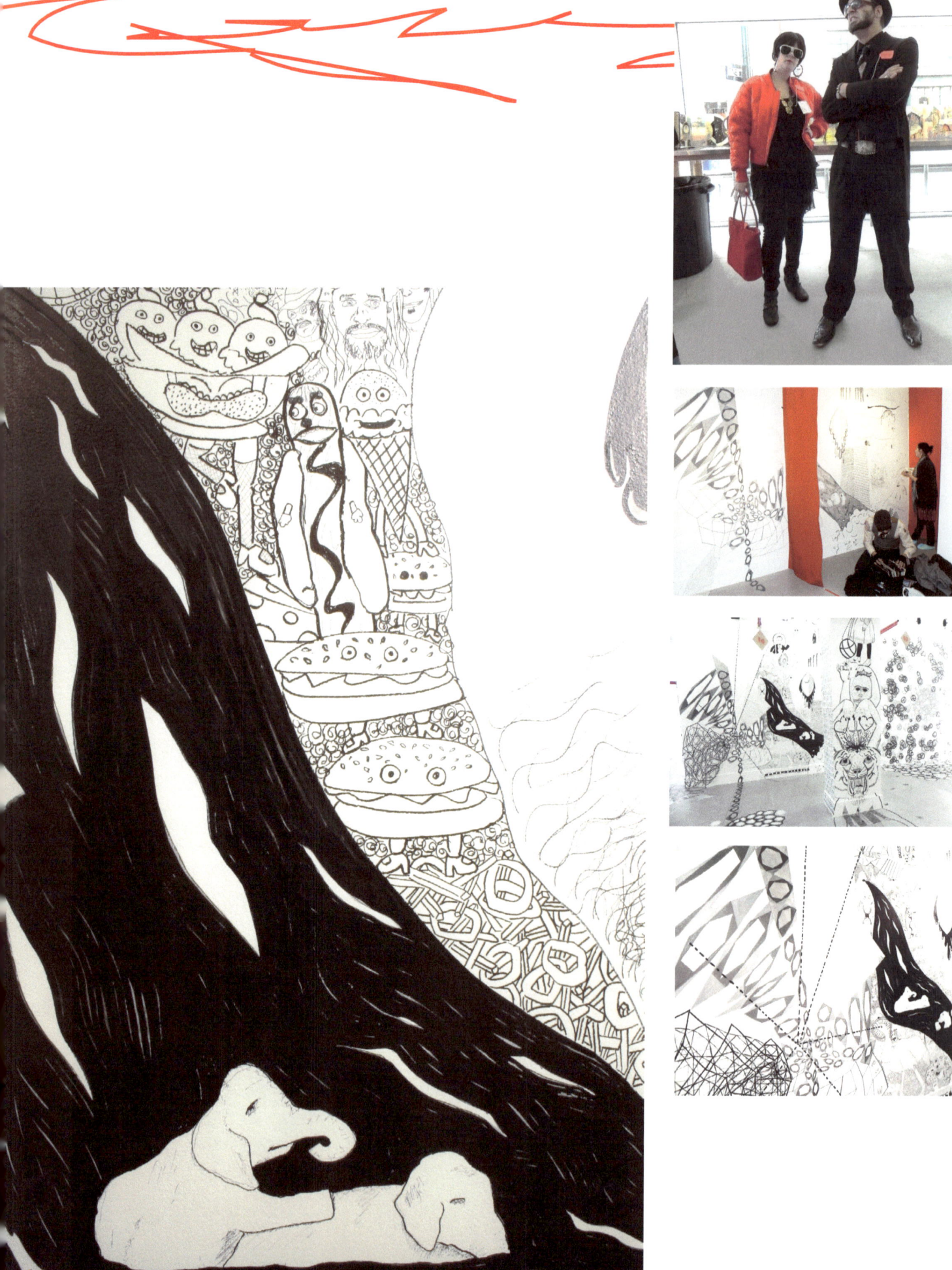

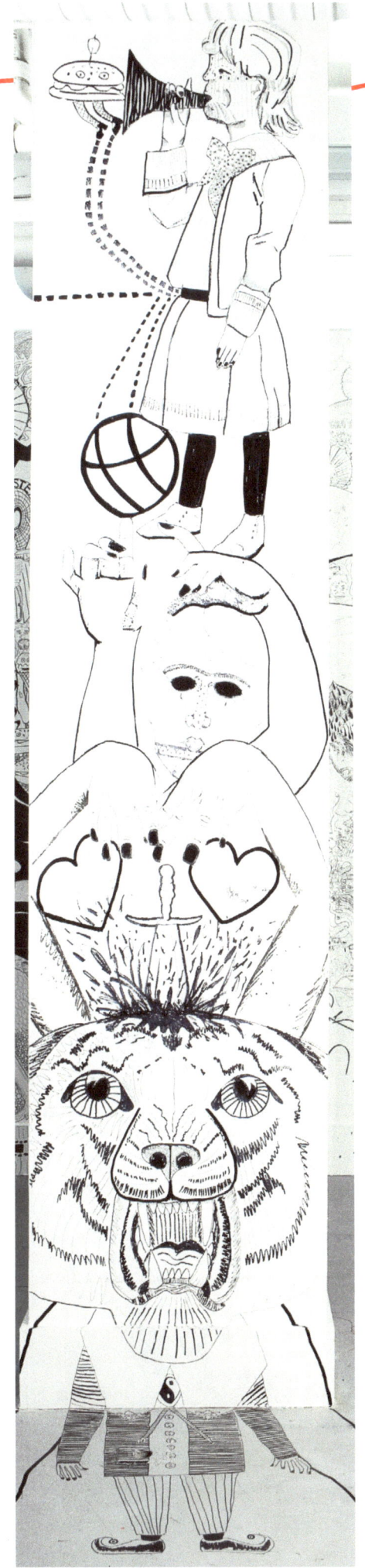

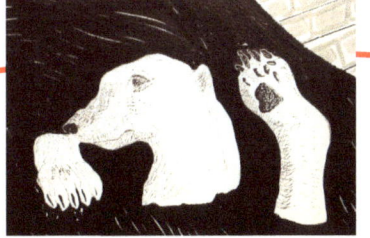
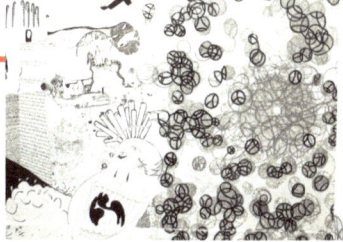

Their account of the work and their participation in Scrawl: "A trio's desperate, and disparate, account of life in the Brass City, born and raised. Chaos and oddities, sound as image … Famed Waterbury landmarks made their Sharpie debut—the suggestive clock tower, sacred Holy Land, the life-giving Naugatuck River, and former mayor and convicted sex offender Philip Giordano. Hidden images abound. Dreams AND nightmares inside of hearts.

"Who is the Sausage Crew? We showed you.

"We had no idea of the degree of madness to anticipate and no preconceived notions of what to expect. We're usually confined to our solitary avenues and are not accustomed to sharing the spotlight.

"We looked at the prescribed projections as doorways into the distinct and universal consciousness of the other artists. Following these paths led us not only into the outer but deeper and deeper into ourselves and our craft. Artistic expressions we never knew existed within ourselves were harnessed as a result of our engagement. There were directions we may not have taken of our own accord had we not encountered these lines.

"There were many memorable moments during our tenure in Scrawl—a college student hit Queen Larita in the head with a microphone while trying to capture the sound of the marker on the wall, while M.C. Sausage yelled, 'More blood, more brain matter, more blood!'; it rained in the gallery, creating chaos. Luckily, none of our angels were disturbed during these unexpected moments."

Larissa Hall/Queen Larita

Key: making things that are visually pleasing, juxtaposition, patterns, humor, anthropomorphism, robot arms, my first monster truck rally—imagery is everywhere. I embrace opportunities for visual confusion. Involvement in the Sausage Crew has challenged my usual creative activities, opening up new opportunities for word-play and theatrics through rap, rather than my history of strictly visual expression.

Hall lives in Woodbridge, CT. She has a degree in Art Education from Southern Connecticut State University. Her Sausage Crew persona, Queen Larita, is an amalgamation of inspiration from many female rappers and musicians she admired in the 1990s, including Queen Latifah, Salt-n-Pepa, and En Vogue.

Mike Pitassi/M.C. Sausage

There are an infinite number of tense, ferocious faces in the world. Everywhere I turn, eyeballs quiver and burst from skulls. There have been an infinite number of times that I've made attempts to ignore them, but sometimes I like to draw them. I would like them to understand how scary they can be. I don't expect that they know about the little sneakers. But sometimes I like to draw them as well. And by them I mean the sneaky little men. They're the ones who embody the mischievous other-worldly forces that are constantly hiding my glasses, keys, wallet, hat, license, shoes, and telephone. Pitassi, the founder of the Sausage Crew, is a musician, performer, and artist who lives in New Haven, CT.

Michael Riley/Dr. BOX

Michael Riley, an artist and musician, lives in New Haven. Among other projects, he plays in two local bands, Eurisko and Bludrum. As the newest member of the Sausage Crew, his most recent creative endeavors have been aimed at creating rap songs. He is greatly inspired by the work of Lil Wayne. Riley has earned a reputation as an artist who can juxtapose the esoteric realities of human existence with the cynicism that plagues an all-too-existentialist art community. His artwork is raw yet tamed, combining elements of hip-hop culture and folk art with an aboriginal flavor. When not performing or creating art, Riley works as a Public Defender in Bridgeport, CT. ■

Jean Scott

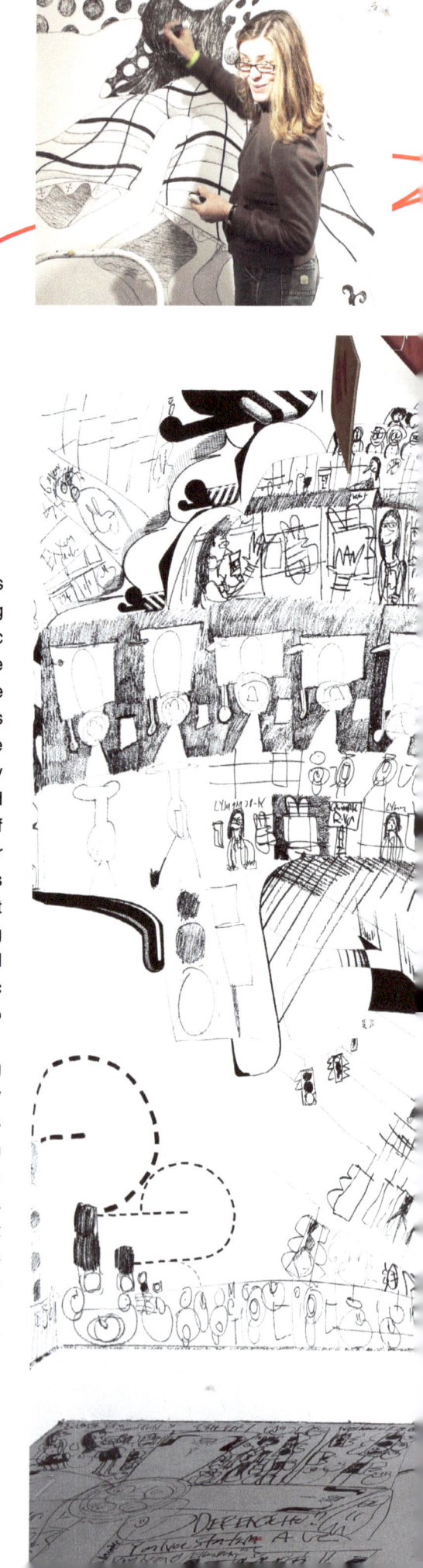

Jean Scott finds images through deliberately subliminal mark-making, focusing on physical and sensory aspects of drawing in order to allow happy accidents. Scott is the only Scrawl artist to title her work, and it plays the rather remarkable trick of being at once very self-contained and complete, while shooting out and relating cunningly to the two teams she had on either side. A consummate Scrawler, Scott used the floor, walls, even the wood bracket the fabric divider descended from, to play her game.

Here is what she writes about *The Magic Beads*: "I started with random marks … When I stepped back, I saw a useful line dividing a large part of the space. Above the line was a somewhat arm-like shape; below it was ... a wolf! The arm clearly had a human body and a head attached to it; I could see the wolf's body extending to the floor. The drawing—and the story—grew from there. The story turned out to be a fairy tale about Grandmother and the Wolf, who encounter each other at the edge of the forest. They struggle together. A newly unmasked character looks on anxiously. He resembles Pinocchio, who has apparently been disguising himself as...Goldilocks? In the background, the Woodcutter rushes onto the scene, but his axe is not raised; instead, he's trying to catch one of the beads that has come loose from Grandma's necklace. These beads have been flung far and wide, floating and falling like magic bubbles, throughout the picture plane and nearly into the viewer's space. At the bottom, we see that strands of the Wolf's luxuriant tail have entangled him with the other figures and also around a nearby tree, all the way up into its branches and across the wall. A mirror image of the Wolf and his surroundings appears on the floor ... but wait: the drawing on the floor shows the Wolf and Grandma not fighting, but instead—embracing! Grandma looks young and desirable, and the Wolf's tail curls and swirls ecstatically. It seems that the magic in the beads has unmasked everyone, to everyone's surprise and delight."

Scott commented about working collectively in the gallery: "It was very interesting to see how other artists approached their work and to hear them express thoughts about it mid-process on a peer-to-peer level; 'shop-talk,' if you will. Some artists were clearly out of their comfort zone, but their occasionally awkward results looked lively and real and exciting, like watching someone stumble on a high wire and then recover: not elegant, but making it across the void …"

Jean Scott graduated summa cum laude from The Maryland Institute, College of Art. She lives and works in Branford, CT, and exhibits in local and national venues. ■

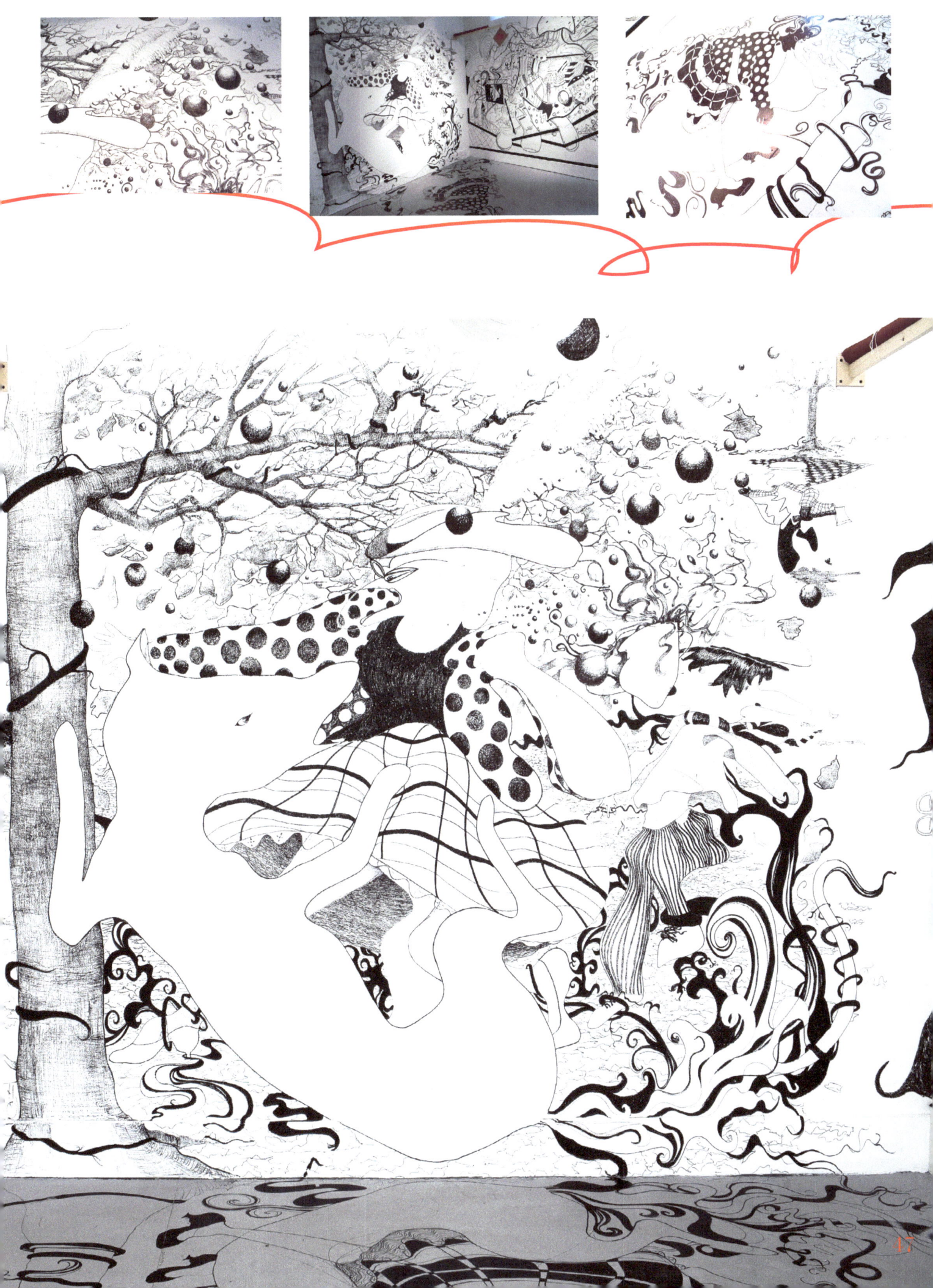

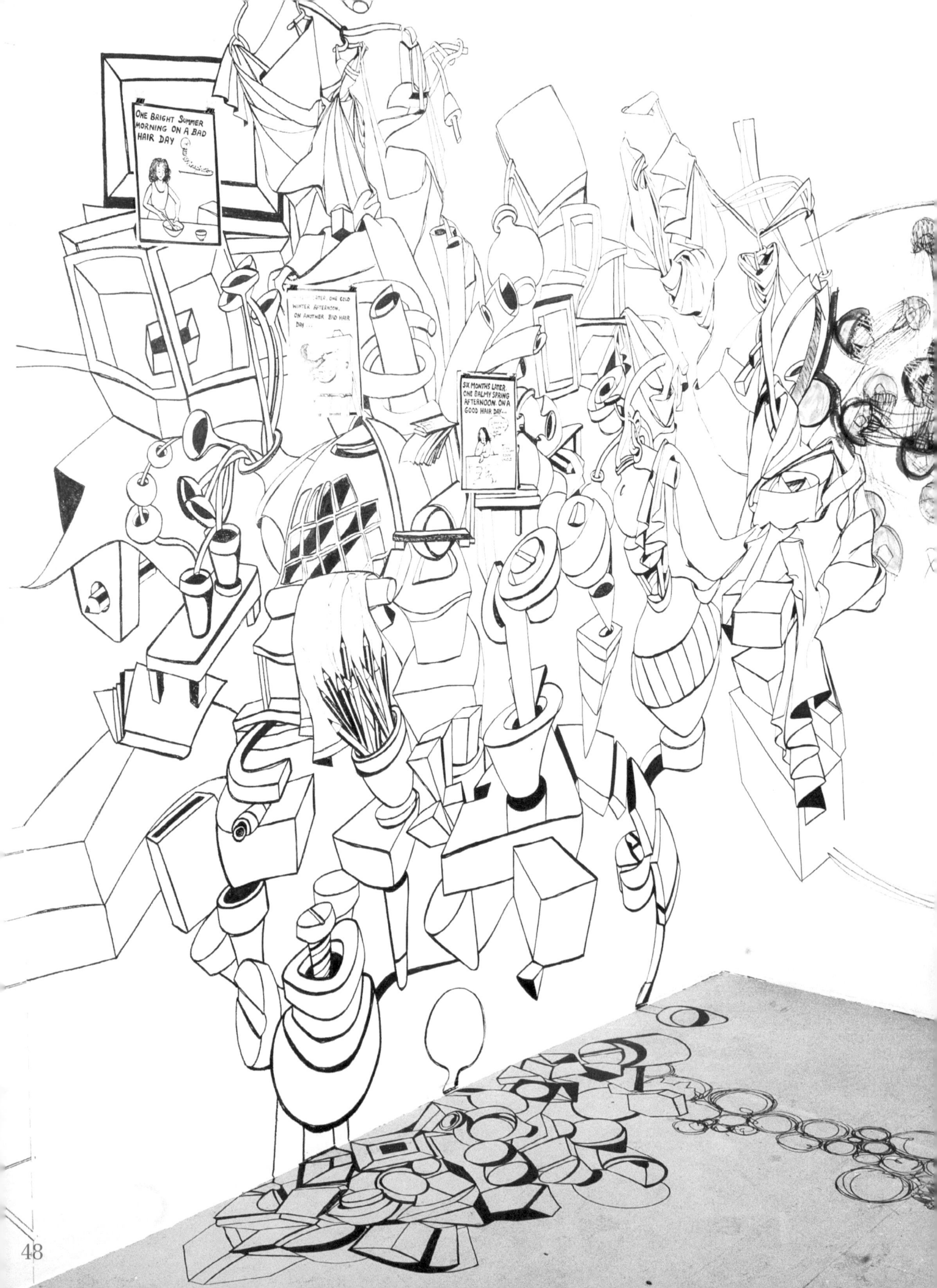

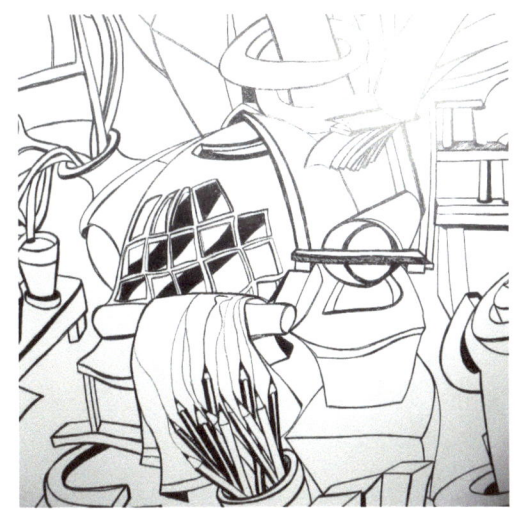

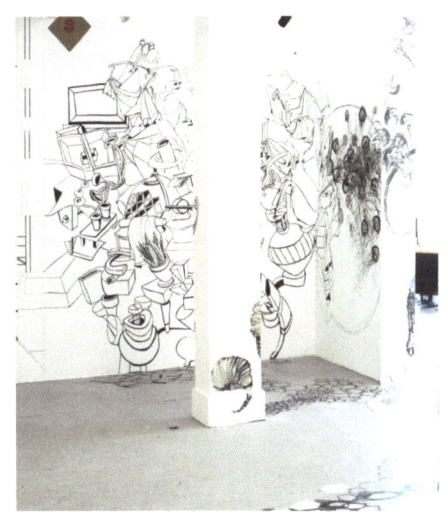

Rashmi Talpade

Rashmi Talpade, whose precise, stacked linear ephemera boldly took over her corner space, was born in Mumbai, India. This cultural heritage infuses her aesthetic, producing work that jointly embraces the images of her upbringing and her home in America. With two worlds vastly different from one another, Talpade accesses the crowded, vertical spaces of Mumbai and the outward expansion of urban sprawl in America. Her swirling, clean-edged drawings of everyday objects deftly comment on the consumerist compulsion to amass possessions found in both developed and developing countries, and the culture of clutter and detritus that exists in both.

She writes of her experience with Scrawl: "Perhaps I did not give it enough thought earlier, but it was quite challenging using Sharpies on the rough wall surface. In retrospect, I should have expected it. However, working on the rough surface, so unlike the smooth paper I usually favor, the character of the line changed and I selected forms which would adapt to the limitations and character of the medium provided.

"Since the drawings were on a large white wall I decided to control my initial urge to fill in dense textural forms and let the line speak for itself. My drawing was like a single line weaving, twisting, traveling, scrawling like a long outline bringing out shapes that I saw in the white surface. Once the drawing emerged, the textures and intricacies became redundant. My drawings celebrate the line as the most dominant force in all arts."

For Scrawl, Talpade enlarged her usual scale and engaged those on either side of her, tackling a difficult and often cramped corner space where she wrestled with curtain

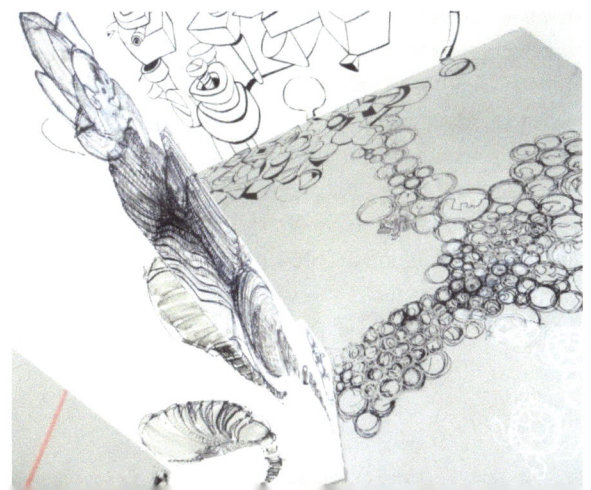

and ladder. Undaunted, the work seemed to pour out of her: images of housewares and office matter boiled over and slid across the wall down to the floor and over to a neighboring column to form a graceful and surprising duet with Alexis Brown's profuse collection of jellyfish, aardvarks, and monkeys. The two parried and comingled with surprising ease and stylistic flow, creating a commentary on abundance—both natural and consumerist—that was witty and delicate.

Rashmi Talpade earned her GD in both fine arts and ceramics from JJ School of Art in India, and is a member of the photographic society of India. In 2006 she was awarded an Artistic Fellowship Grant by the CT Commission on Culture & Tourism. Her work has been commissioned by and is in the permanent collections of, among others, the Roopankar Museum of Modern Art, Bhopal, India; Rotterdam University, Holland; Grindlays International Bank, Mumbai, India; and Middlesex College, CT. Her work has been exhibited in the USA and in India. ■

49

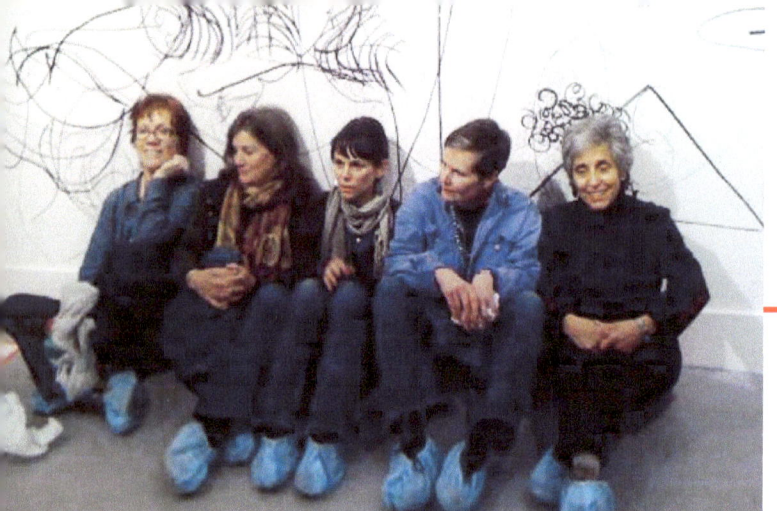

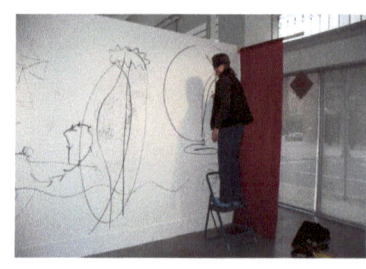

Team Tele:

**Maria Lara-Whelpley, Susan Ferri, Laura Case,
Sylvia Hierro, and Eleanor Tamsky**

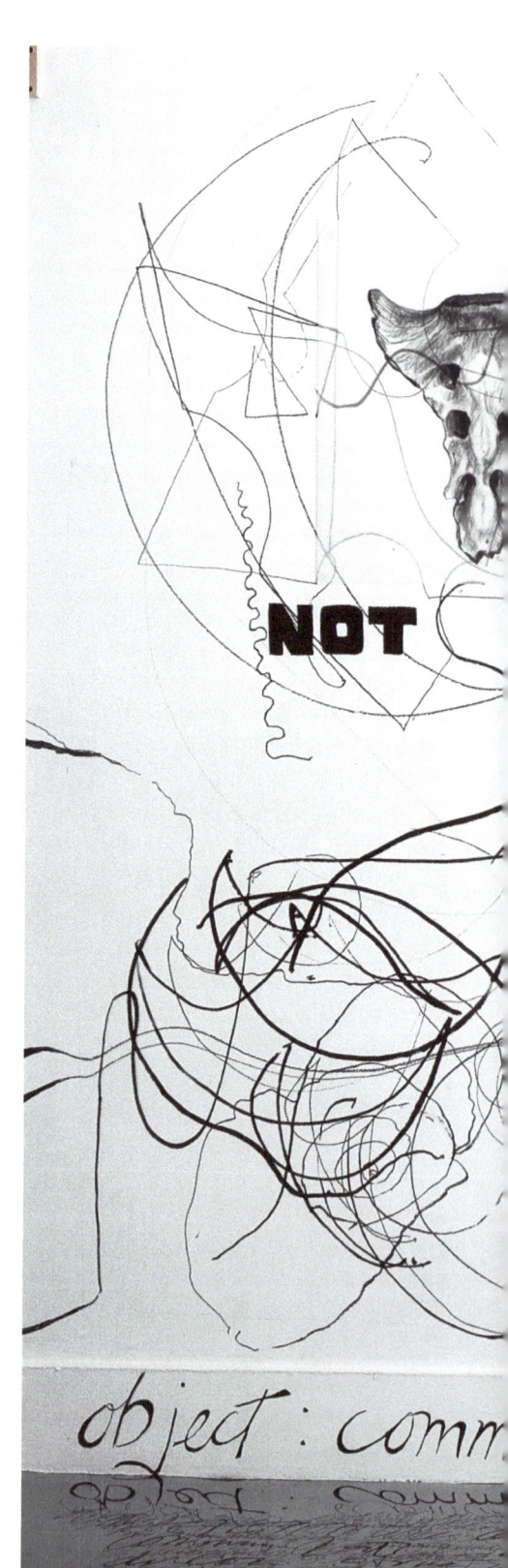

The collaborative work of Team Tele demonstrated the effects of broken communication within a creative context. They deconstructed the act of drawing an unfamiliar object into three areas: seeing and describing a viewed object, hearing the description and then translating it to another, and blindly making the mark that best fit the spoken translation. They then worked in teams with five different objects, over fifteen- to twenty-minute periods. Each object was drawn twice by two separate teams. The "double-blind contour" drawings formed the basis for word-play and traditionally interpreted drawings of each physical object used, informing the viewer of the actual object of the exercise: communication.

Maria: "The entire Scrawl process (collaborative) was novel to me, completely alien to my normal studio practice (alone), and conceptually challenging (installation/time frame as well as Team Tele's emphasis on process versus completed product). All that said, it equaled anything I've done in the past in its insidious and seductive obsessive potential. The most unexpected result (and one of my personal favorites) was the project's undermining of my belief that I communicate well. The creative process we had mapped out had enormous restrictions on the different senses we use while creating. The results forced me to re-examine an entire set of assumptions about how effectively a process or an idea is communicated when our information is restricted—through being blindfolded, receiving complicated instructions over the phone, having to interpret these same instructions, having time limits—and even how successfully we as a culture exchange ideas when we limit our available spectrum of information. Words alone are as incomplete as a charcoal gesture or an interrupted motion sequence—perhaps ideas need all of our senses to be engaged to be understood."

Sylvia: "Since our group worked blindfolded, we were constantly surprised—none of us knew how the work was going to turn out. It was an ongoing adventure that made us aware of how 'the process' was more important that the product. However, one could not predict the energy and excitement our process produced … Because we were blindfolded, our overlapping

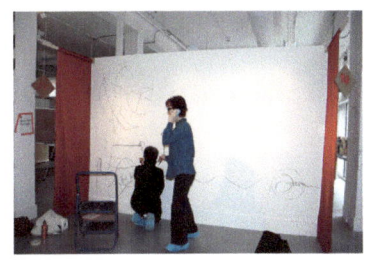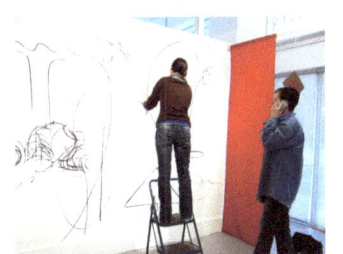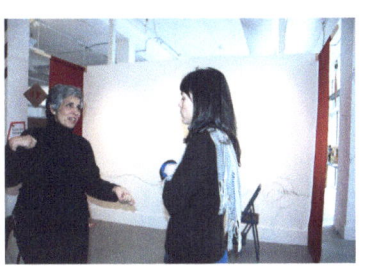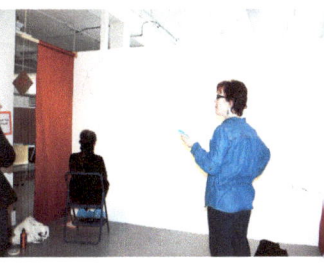

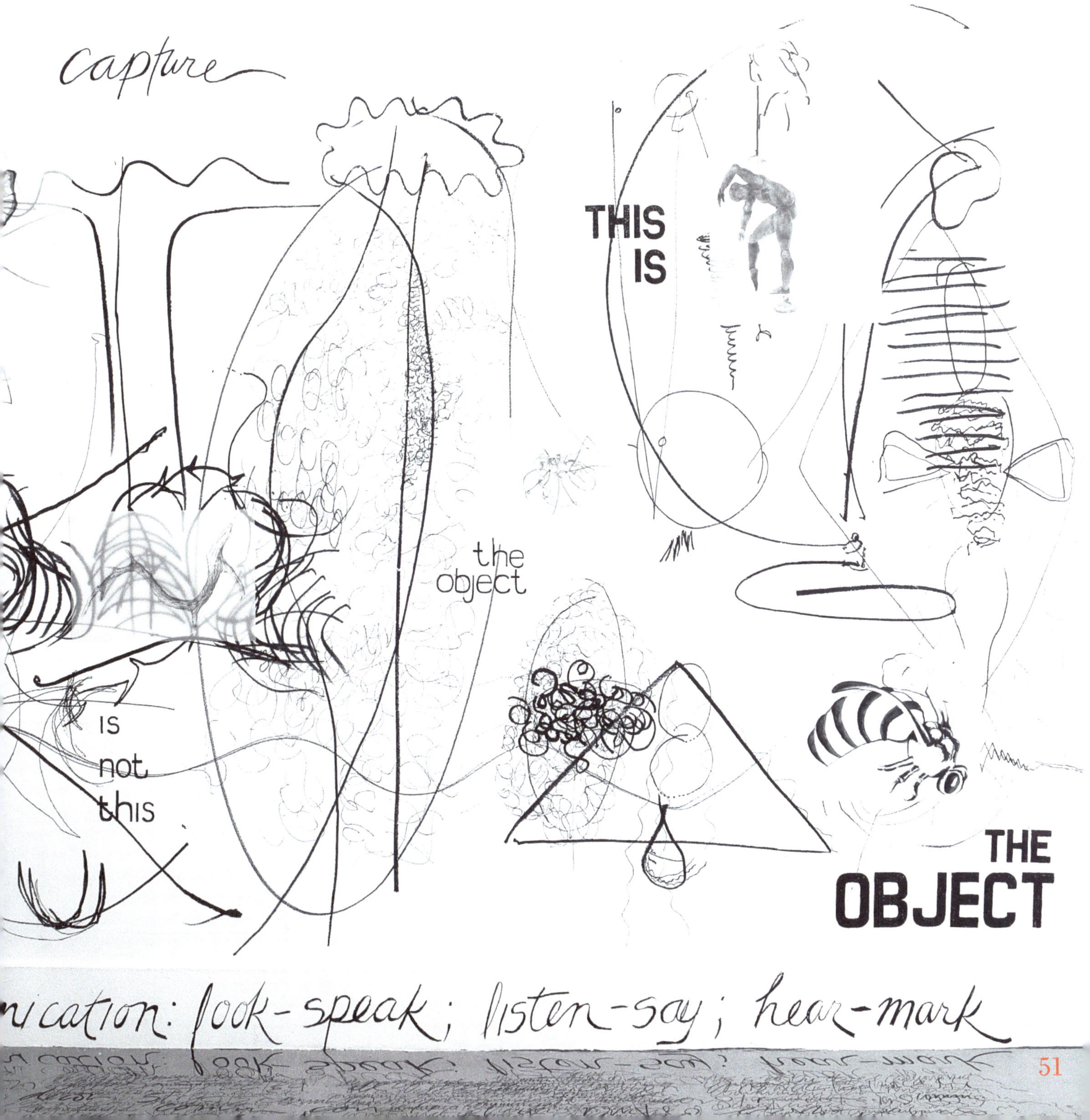

capture

THIS
IS

the
object

is
not
this

THE
OBJECT

...nication: look-speak; listen-say; hear-mark

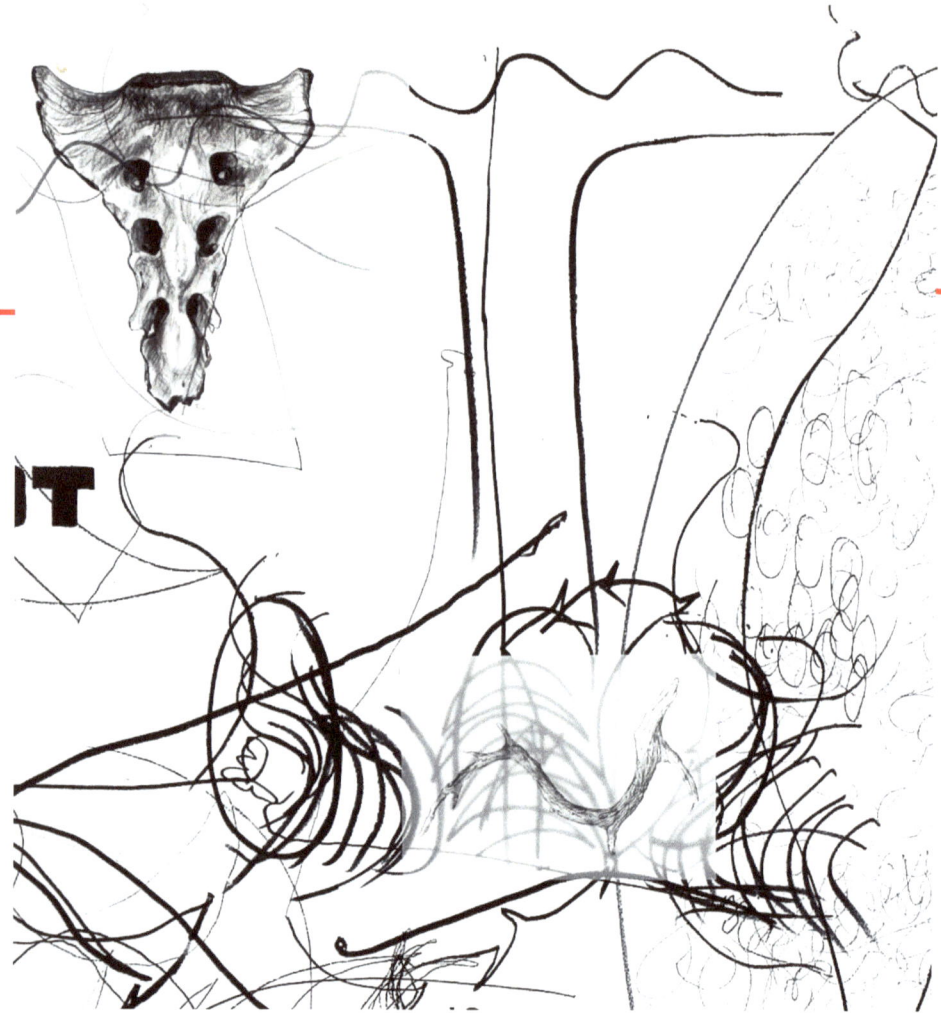

images worked to produce something entirely new and provocative … We left with a desire to do it again ... The open-endedness of the project led to new questions and ideas for another collective project."

Eleanor: "Lately, whenever I hear about a collaborative art project I jump at the opportunity. … Of course, our Team Tele approach to wall drawing was unique in itself and a challenge to all involved. It brought us all together on a visceral level facing our fears and anxieties about drawing on a large scale. Communication, being blindfolded and trusting that we were going to produce a drawing worthy of the Scrawl project. We were a collaborative within a collaborative. Our Team Tele drawing worked well in its own space, but it felt cut off from the whole experience…. Viewing the finished project on opening night was magical. I felt enveloped in the work of art and especially liked the palace

drawing (Andres Madariaga's) where I felt like I could walk right into that world. Everything connected and flowed."

Laura: "My usual studio practice is in a far different discipline (graphic design) and is generally structured by project requirements. Scrawl allowed me (forced me!) to work without requirements other than those dictated by our process and necessitated working in collaboration—something I knew would be a challenge. While each member of the team was certainly outspoken and definite in their views, it was the spontaneity of thought and judgment that developed over the course of the drawing that took me by surprise. Combining five powerful individuals could have resulted in fireworks. Instead, it resulted in laughter, a feeling of accomplishment, a sense of camaraderie and respect.

"I am sure our team process has been described by others. Therefore, I will not

describe the process here other than to say that the role of the 'translator' for the described object to the artist was by far and away the most difficult role—that was an enormous shock."

Maria Lara-Whelpley has a BS in Psychology from the University of Houston, and engaged in graduate studies in Environmental Geology at Wesleyan University. She worked for many years as an Oil Exploration Geophysicist and has taught Science and Spanish. She has studied printmaking, drawing, anatomy, watercolor, and art history variously at the Rowayton Art Center, the Silvermine Guild Art Center, Wooster Art School, Connecticut Graphic Arts, and attended the New York Botanical Garden Extended Studies program in Bronx, NY. In 2008 she created the drawings for a book, The Illustrated Guide to Equine Chiropractic. Lara-Whelpley´s work can be found in private collections across the United States, Mexico, and Europe. She has a studio in New Haven, CT.

Susan Ferri lives and works in New Mexico. She holds an MFA from the International Academy of Art, Santa Fe, and a BA from St. Johns College, Santa Fe. She shows primarily in the southwest and on the west coast. In addition to her own practice of oil painting, Ferri has been a teacher and workshop instructor for over ten years in Santa Fe, Connecticut, and New York.

Laura Case has over twenty-five years' experience designing and creating for publishers, schools, nonprofits, businesses

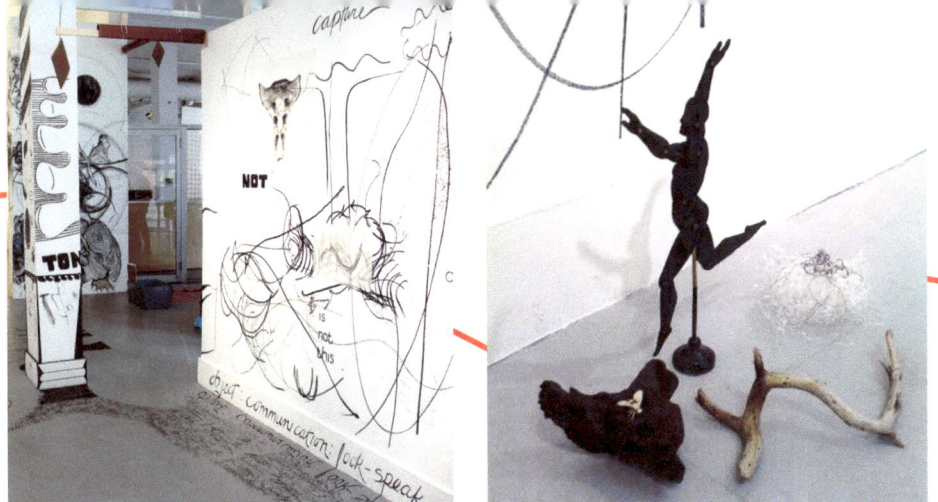

and individuals. A lover of words and type, she works with clients to communicate messages appropriately, genuinely and simply. She is the recipient of numerous professional design awards from AIGA, Connecticut Art Director's Club, Print's Regional Design Annual, and Type Director's Club.

Sylvia Hierro lives and works in Sherman, CT. Her current artistic focus is on organic abstraction, for which employs variously paint, collage, and clay. Hierro earned her BA at Marymount Manhattan College and an MA in Art Education from Southern Connecticut State College. She was the Fine Arts Chair at the Canterbury School in New Milford, CT, for twenty-two years.

Eleanor Tamsky has explored many different media, from glass and metals to ceramics, but in the early 1990s rediscovered her love of oil painting. She has maintained a studio in Mystic, CT, since 1985. Tamsky attended Philadelphia College of Art, Rhode Island School of Design's continuing education program, and Lyme Academy College of Art. She has exhibited her work in Connecticut, Rhode Island, and Massachusetts. ■

THE
OBJECT

on: look-speak; listen-say; hear-mark

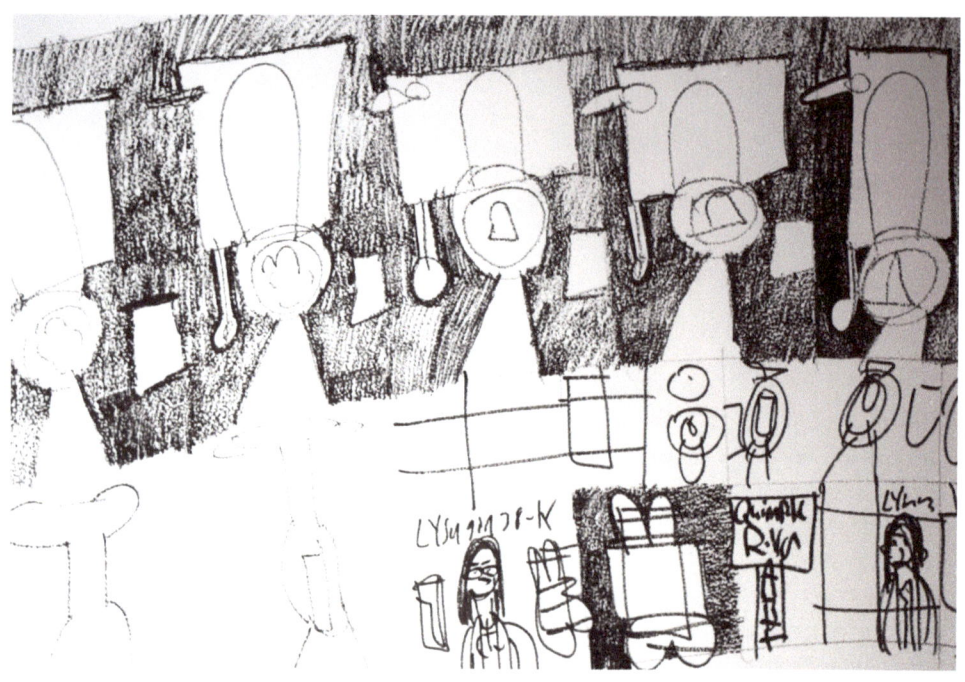

Traffic Lights and Warning Stripes:

Vito Bonnano and Justin Crosby

The team name refers to some of the related objects that inspire the duo: Vito Bonnano often depicts traffic lights, and Justin Crosby has been interested in drawing and painting a rounded, striped shape that he feels certain must have been inspired by the striped, reflective warning panels one sees on the side of the road. Their team identity revolved around the juxtaposition of two divergent interpretations based on similar influences: traffic signage, signals, graffiti, and urban messages. Traffic Lights and Warning Stripes's overarching aesthetic impulse was to create expansive jumbles of their distinct styles with detailed shapes and representational imagery. They collaborated by working simultaneously and building off each other's drawings, creating a vigorous, rhythmic work reflecting the frenetic urban landscape.

Crosby writes of their collaboration: "My partner Vito had endless energy and enthusiasm and was excited to tackle any task involved in executing our drawing. Vito works a lot faster than I do, so occasionally I had to ask him to take a break so I could keep up. We took turns working in all the different sections on the wall and floor, so our images flowed together. It was somewhat difficult due to the different speeds at which my partner and I draw.

"The limitations hindered me, but also pushed me to come up with other solutions. Using markers on textured wall meant that I often had to retrace lines to get them smooth. Filling in large areas of black was also tedious. It was interesting to be able to do a lot of small detail on a relatively large wall because we were limited to markers.

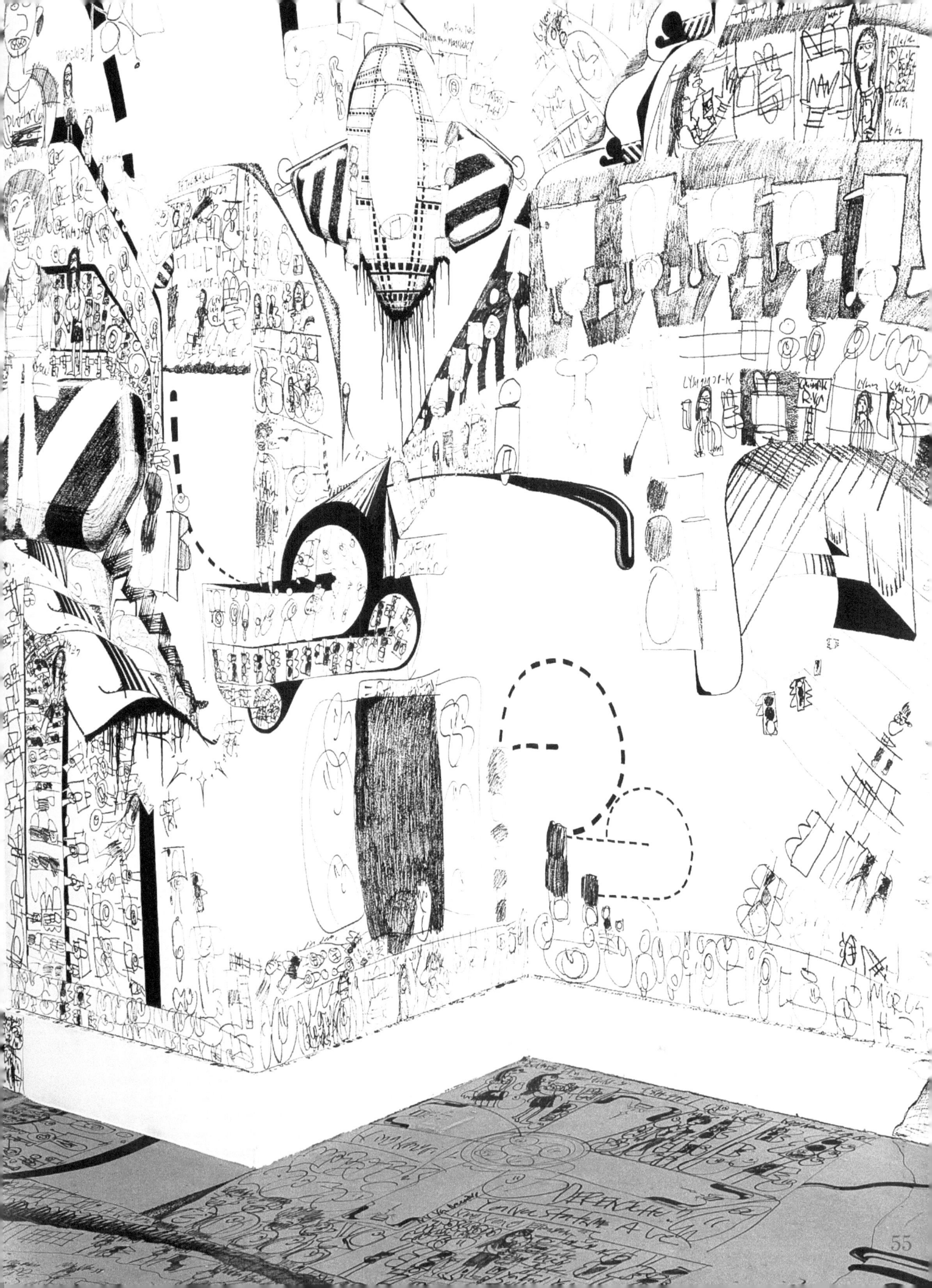

55

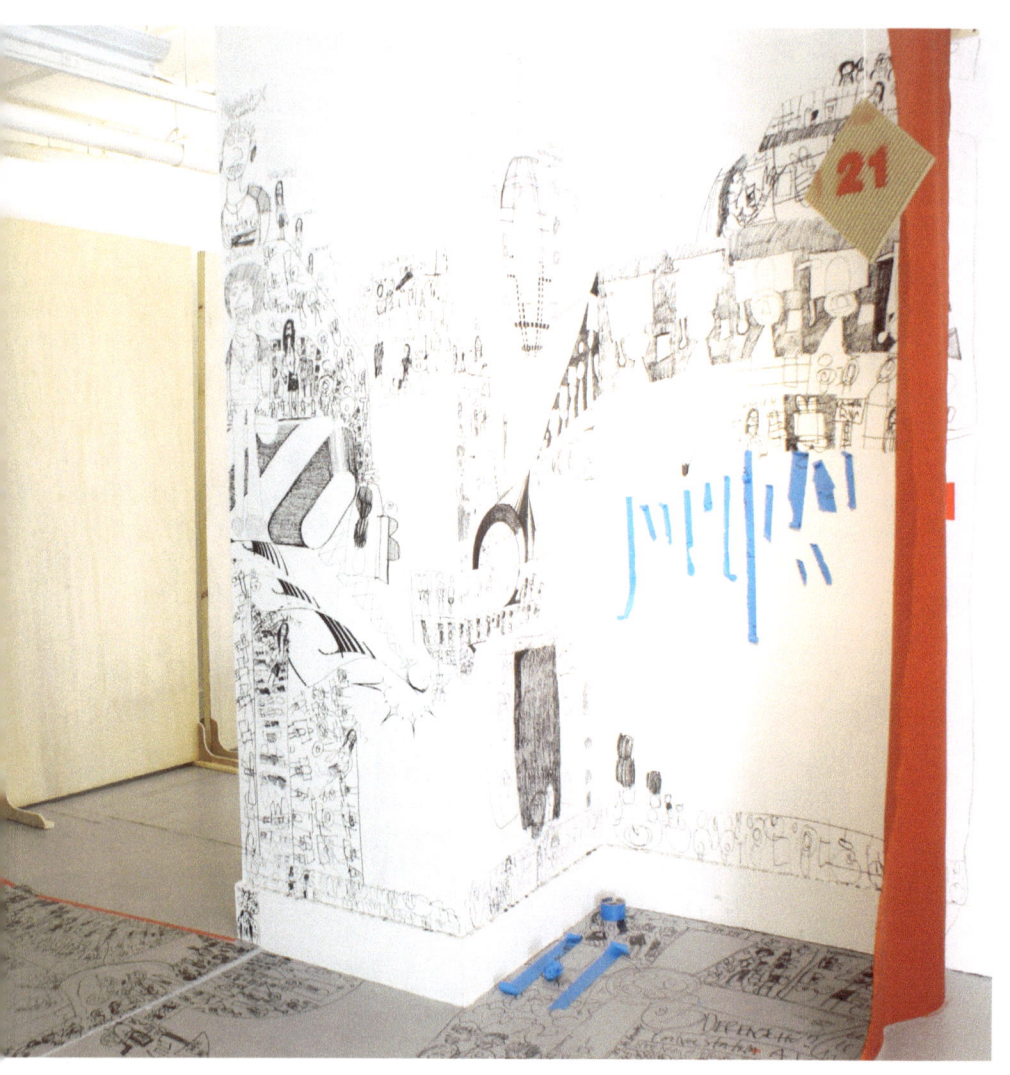

"We let our lines go under the screen into our neighbor's section (Jean Scott); she incorporated those lines into her design, and vice versa."

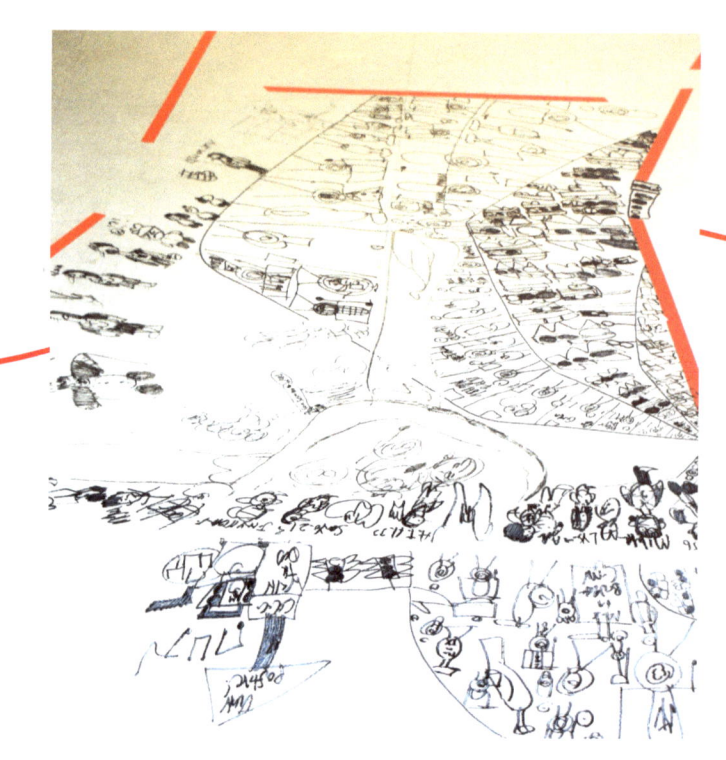

Also … in the absence of different colors, I found myself using multiple different kinds of marks in order to distinguish different parts of my drawing.

"For the overall composition, we balanced areas of dense detail with empty negative spaces. The process was tedious at times, but it ensured that we would be able to get in a lot of detail where we wanted it, and we were quite satisfied with the outcome. We let our lines go under the screen into our neighbor's section (Jean Scott); she incorporated those lines into her design, and vice versa.

"It was usually pretty mellow when we worked, but that was because of scheduling coincidence and not by intention. I didn't feel pressure, but seeing other artists' exciting work motivated me to do good work, too."

Vito Bonnano began to create artwork based on his dreams at age fourteen. As a highly functioning autistic adult, he relies on drawing to assist him in getting out his internal feelings. He finds that his condition helps him remember specific places and incidents with great detail, which is reflected in his drawings. Bonnano has participated in the Bridgeport Arts Festival and shown at Umbrella Arts, New York; Read's Art Space, Bridgeport, CT; Creative Arts Workshop, New Haven, CT; the AWE in Autism project; Davenport College Gallery at Yale University, New Haven, CT; Nest Arts Factory, Bridgeport, CT; and had a solo exhibition at Eastern Connecticut State College. His work has been included in both ArtHamptons and the Outsider Art Fair.

Justin Crosby has worked on collaborative murals, been a teacher, and is now focusing on his art-making full time. Rather than presuming to offer answers, Crosby's artwork presents viewers with a fantastic space that invites them to engage their imagination and experiences in order to form their own unique interpretations. ■

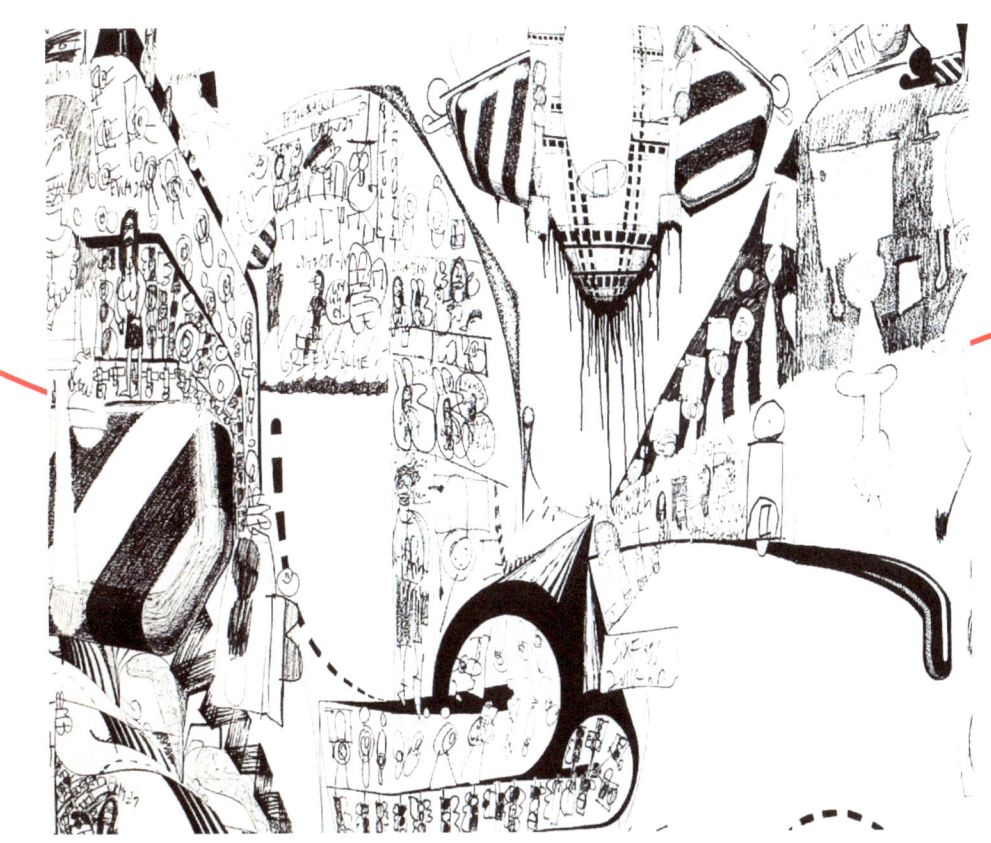

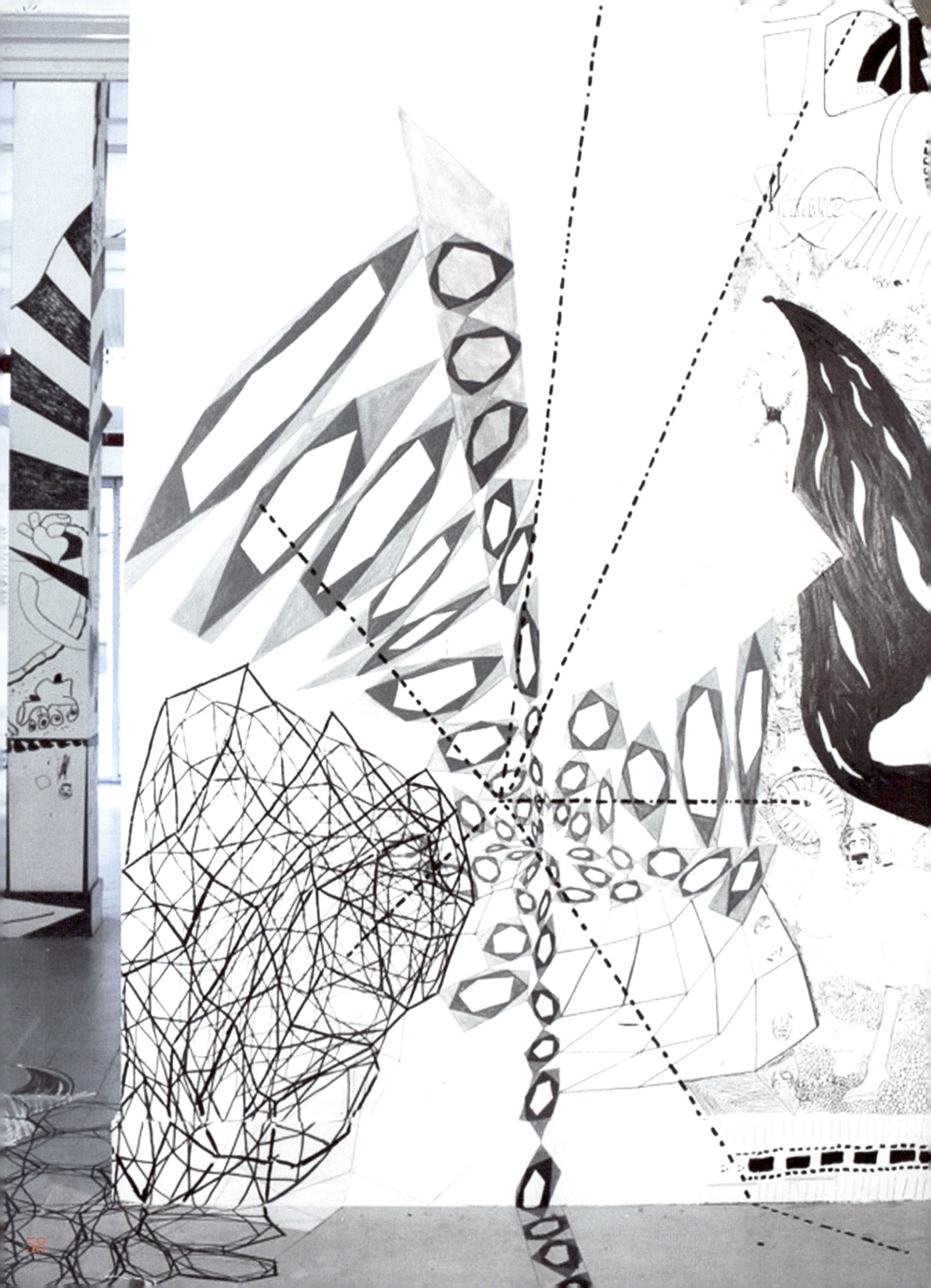

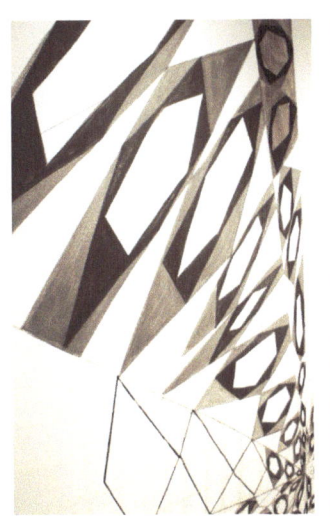
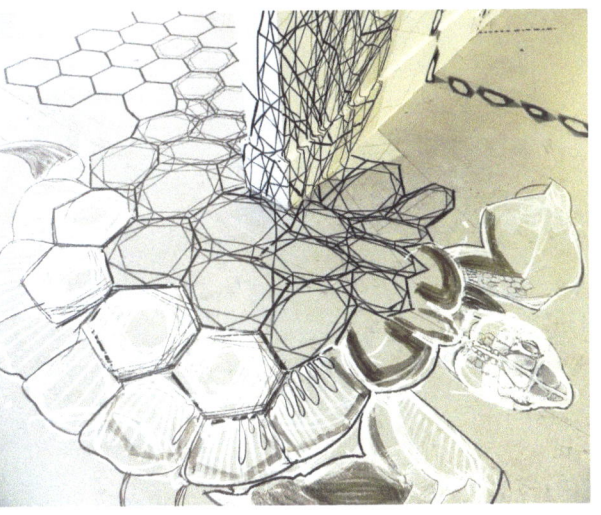

Laura Watt

Laura Watt used Sharpies and a variety of paint markers to construct a radiating geometric web which wrapped around her wall space and spanned a portion of the floor. Like much of her output, it evoked quilt patterns, Tantric diagrams, and playing with various tropes of modernist geometric abstraction, all while engaging the space around her. At once stand-alone with a striking visual impact, her work jostled and meshed with neighbors whose work accessed entirely different threads of thought and mark-making.

The Philadelphia-based artist's visits to the space were not impromptu and her time was limited, therefore she arrived focused and with a plan. Here is what she says about the experience in relation to her usual practice:

"… I worked in a more improvised way. I came with an idea of what I wanted to do on the wall—had drawing structures that I wanted to use—but found, once in the space, that I was using different structures than I intended to. This was great, as I got to see how drawing vocabularies interacted with each other."

Watt's work, a seemingly self-contained nexus able to span infinitely across space, was disrupted at the margins, where she met with wildlife (turtles, cranes) and segued across into Rodriguez's grand entrance arch.

"I found the whole to be really engrossing, the entirety of the show was a grand statement, while the juxtapositions between one artist's work and another made you want to move in for a slower, longer, closer look. The limitations helped create the gestalt of the show."

Watt's work explores the possibilities of abstract content as found in pattern and color. She finds they offer ways to address the modernist endgame that painting still finds itself playing, while simultaneously evoking a much larger and diverse group of art and craft forms. Watt is a graduate of Yale University and Bennington College and a recipient of The Helen Winternitz Award. She is currently represented by McKenzie Fine Art, New York, and has exhibited at Locks Gallery, Philadelphia; The Phillips Museum, Lancaster, PA; and The Aldrich Contemporary Art, Museum, Ridgefield, CT, among other venues. Her work has been written about by ARTPULSE, Arts Magazine, Philadelphia Weekly, The Village Voice, Culturecatch.com, and the ARTBLOG. ■

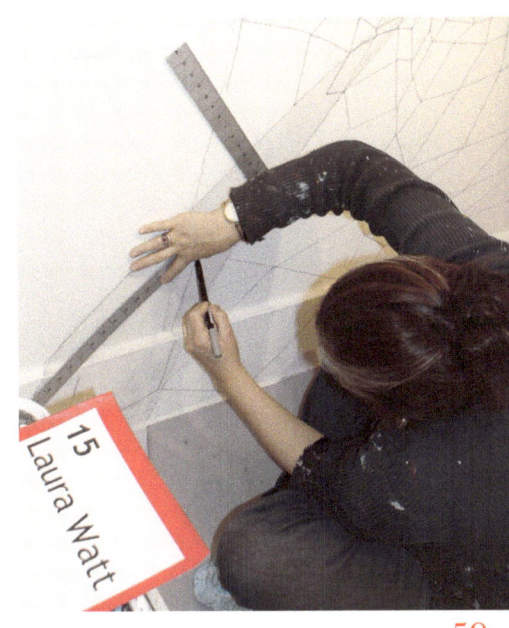

Acknowledgments

I want to extend my deepest gratitude for the Andy Warhol Foundation's continued support for our exhibitions. The general operating support from the Community Foundation of Greater New Haven comes at a time when many organizations, Artspace included, feel particularly vulnerable, and their help provided a cushion on which to plan expanded outreach, from drawing classes for Vets and NHPS students, to offsite gatherings in pubs, to yoga-inspired live drawing, and partnerships with several museums.

The Eli Whitney Museum practically leapt at the chance to work with Martha, who is a kindred spirit of the Museum's Director, Bill Brown. With his usual pluck, Bill roped in master carpenter-cum-boat builder Mike Dunn and recruited Museum apprentices, who honed their woodworking skills over winter break while building the handsome and re-usable screens that allowed artists to work in relative privacy when they wished. We are also grateful to the Yale Center for British Art and The Aldrich Contemporary Art Museum for their enthusiastic and collaborative support. It is a particular pleasure for me to have Artspace serve as a New Haven site for The Aldrich's Draw On! festival.

Scrawl serves as a reminder that in fiscally lean times it is possible to produce outstanding art and artistic meaning on a shoestring, with nothing more than shoe leather—or hospital booties!—and ingenuity. It certainly could not have happened without the countless hours contributed by all the participating artists, to whom we owe a great deal of gratitude. Other thanks are due, in particular, to Jock Reynolds, Robert Post, Suzanne Enser-Ryan, Richard Klein, James Esber, Laura Spinelli, Colin Burke, Rebecca Salter, and Meredith Miller, who through their individual support and generosity, each helped make Scrawl more ambitious and exciting.

Helen Kauder

Scrawl was a labor of love. To make this juggernaut run smoothly, all the Artspace staff and volunteers, and friends from outside institutions worked exceedingly hard. I am more than grateful to them—this truly was a team effort, and I feel privileged to have had the chance to work with such a fine group. Scrawl would be nothing without the artists in the exhibition, who selflessly gave their time and talents. I would also like to personally thank Helen Kauder, Artspace's director, for thinking that Scrawl was not only OK to do, but a good idea, and for all of her support, suggestions, and good will along the way. Thanks for taking the leap. There is no way to repay properly all of the effort that so many put into this exhibition. I will try anyway (please see below) and am eternally grateful to those who gave so freely of their talents to make this happen.

Martha Lewis

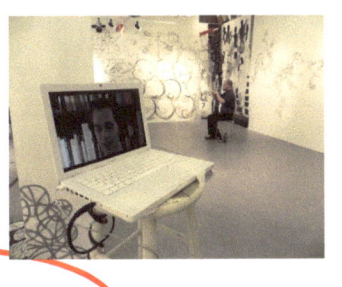
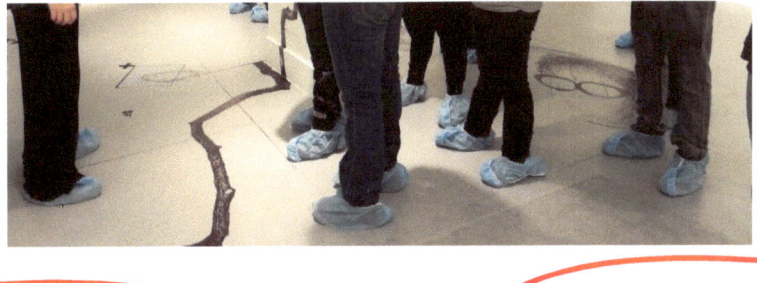

Helen and Martha together would like to thank:

All of our wonderful interns, volunteers, and helpers for their tireless hard work on Scrawl: Colin Burke, Joy Daniels, Alyssa Denning, Sara Guzzo, Caleb Hendrickson (particularly for his help with Scrawl TV), Cecily Hughes, Kiku Langford, Alana Moreno, Carissa Perez, Shelli Stevens, Paul Theriault, Lucy Topaloff, and Jeremy Wolin.

A huge thank you to Courtney McCarroll, without whose patience and organizational skills Scrawl never would have happened, and who helped make The Big Reveal such a success. Alexis Zanghi, who helped with everything from PR to drinks, and all the concepts in-between: your participation was invaluable. This catalogue has been beautifully designed by Janice Brunell, who knew exactly what Martha wanted without her having to coherently verbalize it—grazie mille.

A loud round of applause to Kevin Stevens and all of the Scrawl artists who came to prepare the gallery walls in the snowstorms before Scrawl, and those who helped paint over the walls and floors afterwards. A special shout out goes to Meaghan Monaghan, who elegantly kept our artists' schedules organized so we knew who was coming and when, at all times; she is impeccable, and a delight to work with.

We really cannot give enough thanks to the design team of Maegen McElderry and Stephanie Rogowski for their tireless and imaginative help with Scrawl's conceptual and physical underpinnings and their exquisite (truly) model of the space. They went above and beyond the call every time and were incredibly fun to work with as well. Thanks also to Alexis Brown for her wise counsel, amazing posters, T-shirts, and conceptual munificence with so many aspects of this project.

Meredith Miller, Larissa Hall, Rashmi Talpade, Ken Lovell, Kerry O'Grady and the Artspace interns all gave us wonderful photographs to use for this catalogue; the images are, of course, vital—THANK YOU.

We would also like to thank our amazing institutional collaborators: Scrawl really found a terrific sponsor in Newell/Rubbermaid, who make the Sharpie/Expo and Prismacolor brands. They generously donated our art supplies and were just delightful to work with. We are so grateful for their willingness to play our game with us!

Big thanks to Kristen Michels and our friends at Sharpie, Prismacolor, and Expo; Shawn Szirbik from Hull's Art Supplies; Robert Post; Suzanne Enser-Ryan and her team at The Aldrich Museum for generously partnering with us in so many innovative ways; Ray Pagliaro from Joe's Paint for the gorgeous Scrawl fabric and paint; Dr. William Rosenblatt for the hospital booties; Peg Oliveira and Heidi Sormaz, our neighbors at Fresh Yoga, for their free session in our space. Enormous thanks to Bill Brown and Mike Dunn at the Eli Whitney Museum; Cyra Levenson from the Yale Center for British Art; Suzannah Holsenbeck and Kyle Sklar from the Coop Arts & Humanities High School, who made our collaboration with Rebecca Salter and the school possible; Karen Dow and the administration at Educational Center for the Arts, for making the participation of her team, the Futurists, possible; and all of the SCRAWL-TV artists who each, through their individual support and generosity, helped make Scrawl happen.

Helen Kauder and Martha Lewis

Scrawl was made possible by in-kind support from the following Newell-Rubbermaid companies:

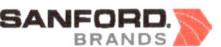

PRISMACOLOR®

Sharpie®

EXPO®

Scrawl is proud to be a part of The Aldrich Museum's Draw On! festival.

Artspace is grateful for the support it receives from the Andy Warhol Foundation for the Visual Arts, the City of New Haven Office of Economic Development, the Connecticut Commission on Culture & Tourism, the Community Foundation for Greater New Haven, New Alliance Foundation, TD Bank, Yale University, Yale/New Haven Hospital, and individual Friends of Artspace.

ARTSPACE
50 Orange Street • New Haven CT 06510
203.772.2709 • www.artspacenh.org

Scrawl artists:

Cat Balco, Anna Broell Bresnick, Alexis Brown, Francis Cooke, The Futurists: Karen Dow & her 12 students from the Educational Center for the Arts ,Laura Gardner, Zachary Keeting, Ken Lovell, Andres Madariaga, Melissa Marks, Maegen McElderry, Tim Nikiforuk, Kerry O'Grady, Rebecca Salter - in collaboration with students from the Cooperative Arts & Humanities High School, The Sausage Crew: Queen Larita, M.C. Sausage, and Dr. BOX, Daniel Rios Rodriguez, James Rose, Jean Scott, Rashmi Talpade, Team Tele: Maria Lara-Whelpley, Sylvia Hierro, Laura Case, Eleanor Tamsky, & Susan Ferri, Traffic Lights and Warning Stripes Team: Vito Bonnano and Justin Crosby, Laura Watt

ScrawlTV artists:

Brad Amorosino, Giada Crispiels, Peter Konsterlie , Luiza Kurzyna, Heather Lawless, Melissa Marks, John Odonnell, Nick Primo, Shane Savage-Rumbaugh, Clinton Stringer, Joey Fauerso, Lisa Malone

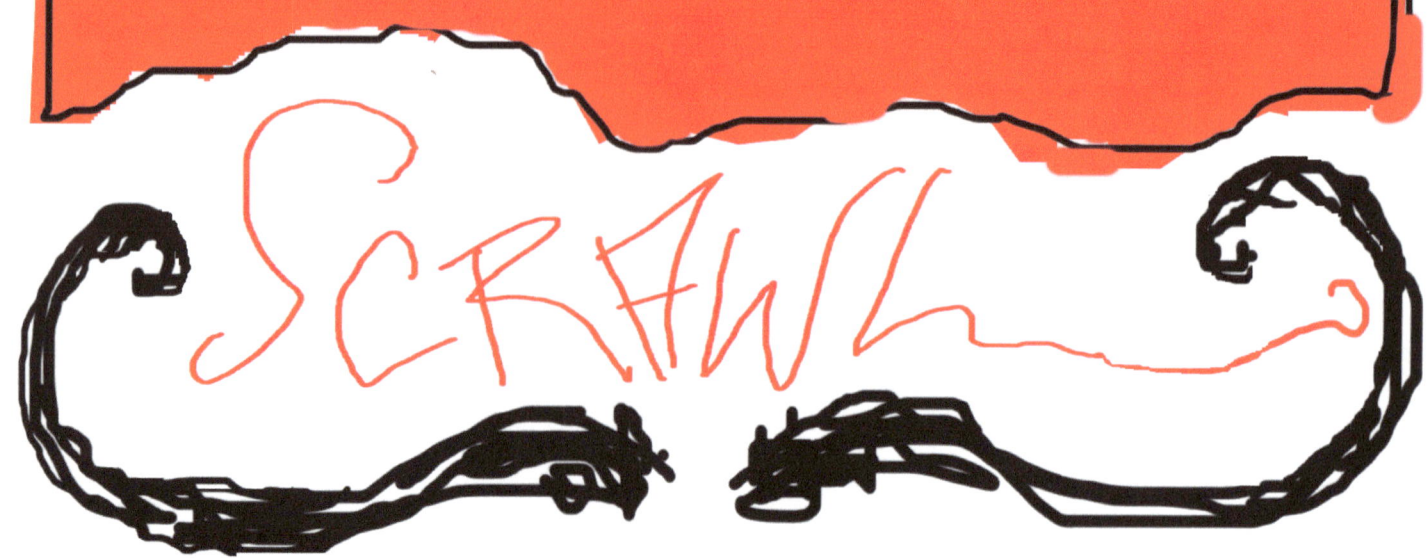

www.ingramcontent.com/pod-product-compliance
Lightning Source LLC
Chambersburg PA
CBHW051048180526
45172CB00002B/554